GREEK ORACLES

ROBERT FLACELIERE

GREEK ORACLES

Translated by
DOUGLAS GARMAN

ELEK BOOKS
ALL SAINTS STREET LONDON

English translation © Elek Books Limited 1965

Published by
ELEK BOOKS LIMITED
2 All Saints Street, London, N.1

and simultaneously in Canada by
The Ryerson Press
299 Queen Street West, Toronto, 2B

Originally published under the title DEVINS ET ORACLES GRECS
by Presses Universitaires de France, Paris, 1961
© 1961, *Presses Universitaires de France*

PRINTED IN GREAT BRITAIN
in 12 on 13 pt Fournier type
BY UNWIN BROTHERS LIMITED
WOKING AND LONDON

CONTENTS

LIST OF PLATES

The Publishers gratefully acknowledge the sources of the illustrations appearing in this volume:

J. Allan Cash, 1

Photographie Giraudon, 2, 11, 12

Alinari, 3

Department of Antiquities, Berlin, 4, 5, front of jacket

British Museum, 6, 7

Hirmer Fotoarchiv, 8, 10, 14, back of jacket

Agora Excavations, 9

SCR Photo Library, 15

FOREWORD

Man is regarded as being an animal endowed with reason. But is reason in all circumstances a sufficient guide to conduct? There are still plenty of books being published today with titles such as *The Key to Your Dreams*, fortune-tellers are not short of clients and many people believe in astrology and horoscopes. Nevertheless, there are not many countries where soothsayers and sorcerers are still publicly honoured for their contribution to the common good, and those countries where they are, like Africa or Tibet, are usually considered to be backward.

In antiquity divination was esteemed as an official institution. Everywhere, in Egypt and Mesopotamia, even in Israel and later in Rome, it was obligatory for political and military leaders to consult the oracle, to 'take the auspices', before embarking upon any enterprise unless they were prepared to be accused of irresponsibility or, in case of failure, of having omitted to seek guidance from the gods.

It was the ancient Greeks who invented philosophy, and Socrates who 'brought it down from heaven to earth'. They harshly criticized the most sacred traditions and are regarded with every justification as having been the founders of rationalism. Yet in their attitude to divination were they any different from other ancient peoples? What, in particular, was their attitude to the irrational that lies at the heart of the belief in oracles?

The purpose of this book[1] is to attempt to answer such questions.

[1] Although it is out of date on a number of questions the basic work on the subject remains: A. Bouché-Leclercq, *Histoire de la divination dans l'Antiquité*, 4 vols., Paris, 1879–82. The standard English work is: H. W. Parke and D. E. Wormell, *The Delphic Oracle*, 2 vols., 2nd ed., Oxford University Press, 1956.

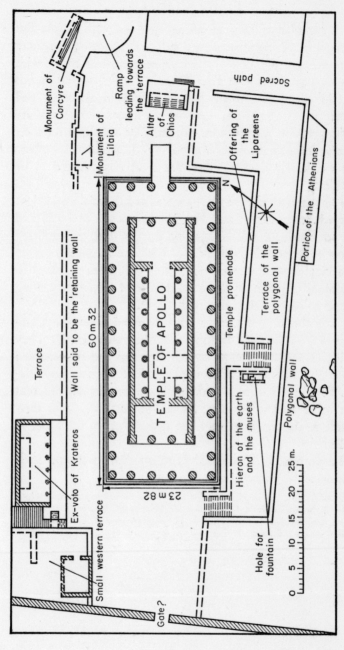

The Temple of Apollo and terrace at the end of the fourth century. Restored plan

Monument of Corcyre

Ramp leading towards the terrace

Monument of Lilaia

Altar of Chios

Sacred path

Offering of the Lipareens

Portico of the Athenians

Terrace

Wall said to be the 'retaining wall'

60 m 32

N

TEMPLE OF APOLLO

Temple promenade

Terrace of the polygonal wall

Ex-voto of Krateros

23 m 82

Hieron of the earth and the muses

Polygonal wall

Small western terrace

Hole for fountain

Gate?

0 5 10 15 20 25 m.

DIVINATION BY SIGNS

At the beginning of his treatise *De Divinatione*, Cicero says: 'It is an ancient belief, going back to heroic times but since confirmed by the unanimous opinion of the Roman people and of every other nation, that there exists within mankind an undeniable faculty of divination. The Greeks called it *mantike*, that is the capacity to foresee, to know future events, a sublime and salutary act that raises human nature most nearly to the level of divine power. In this respect, as in many others, we have improved upon the Greeks by giving this faculty a name derived from the word god, *divinatio*, whereas according to Plato's explanation the Greek word comes from *furor* (*mania* from which *mantike* is derived). What cannot be gainsaid is that there is no nation, whether the most learned and enlightened or the most grossly barbarous, that does not believe that the future can be revealed and does not recognize in certain people the power of foretelling it.'

Thus in Cicero's view divination is the revelation of the future, the knowledge of what is to come. Can we accept this definition? In the first place it is important to note that there are some future events that can be foreseen by the unaided human intelligence. When an astronomer predicts an eclipse— as Thales of Miletus succeeded in doing as long ago as the sixth century B.C.—he does not rely upon divination. His ability to foretell the position of the sun, the moon and the earth at a particular date in the future is due solely to his knowledge of the movements of the stars and his ability to calculate: it is in no sense the result of revelation or of irrational intuition.

Does this mean, then, that divination implies simply a supernatural knowledge of the future? Certainly this is its essential function, since it is usually with respect to the future that oracles and soothsayers are consulted. Quite often, however, they were also asked questions about the past or the present. In Sophocles' *Oedipus the King*, Oedipus first of all sends Creon to the oracle at Delphi to find out what can *immediately* be done to free Thebes from the horror of the plague. The reply that Creon brings back from Apollo is that the murderer of King Laios must be punished since it is the defilement resulting from this murder that is causing the plague. Whereupon Oedipus calls upon the seer Tiresias to use every resource of his art in order to reveal this secret from the *past*: Who was it that had killed Laios?

Here, as in many other cases, divination is related to those practices of expiation, purification and exorcism which the Greeks summed up in a word originally borrowed from medicine: *katharsis*. The purpose of katharsis was to ensure that society (in this case the city of Thebes) or individuals (for example Orestes in Aeschylus' *Eumenides*) should be delivered from the consequences of a crime committed in the past. In cases such as this, where the seer was seeking to recover from the shadowy past some sin of which the guilty man, though suffering from its effects, was himself ignorant, it might almost be said that divination in association with katharsis was the forerunner of modern methods of psychoanalysis, in much the same way as astrology was of astronomy.

In order, therefore, to include those many instances where it was concerned with the past, and especially with the present, we may perhaps say that divination means supernatural knowledge of what is otherwise unknowable. As Cicero notes, the Latin word *divinatio* clearly indicates that it is an activity closely connected with divine matters and is also an essential part of religion, for the etymology of the word makes it applicable to all aspects of religion. Above all divination assumes belief in a providence that is concerned with the lot of humanity and is prepared to help men by revealing what would otherwise be unknown to them.

Generally speaking, in ancient times the stronger the spirit of religion the greater the importance men accorded to divination. Bouché-Leclercq has even maintained that 'divination was perhaps the most vital aspect of the religion of Greece and Rome'. Indeed it was continually concerned with the everyday affairs of private individuals as well as with the acts of statesmen. As regards the latter, the most significant example is that of the Athenian Nicias, to whom Plutarch devotes one of his *Lives*. Here is how Fustel de Coulanges summed up that life in his *La Cité Antique*, where he treats it precisely from our point of view: 'Nicias belonged to a great and wealthy family. . . . While the Athenian people were debating the Sicilian expedition Nicias took the floor and declared that both his priests and his soothsayer had discovered omens against the expedition. But since the oracles pronounced by Alcibiades' soothsayers were to the opposite effect the people remained undecided. While things were at this stage some men returned from Egypt, where they had been to consult the god Ammon, then much in vogue. The oracle they had brought back declared: "The Athenians will capture all the Syracusans." Whereupon the people at once declared themselves in favour of the war and, despite his reservations, Nicias was appointed to lead the expedition. Before setting out he performed the customary sacrifice. Like every other general, he was accompanied by a bevy of soothsayers and sacrificial priests. . . . But so many extraordinary events foretold disaster that he had little hope of success: crows had defiled a statue of Pallas; a man had mutilated himself on an altar; the expedition had set out during the unpropitious period of the Plynteria. Nicias knew only too well that this war would prove fatal to him and his country. Throughout the whole course of the campaign he always appeared to be wary and timorous, scarcely daring to order an assault. . . . The Greeks failed to take Syracuse and after suffering severe losses the decision was taken to return to Athens. Nicias prepared his fleet for the homeward journey; the sea was still free. But there was an eclipse of the moon. He consulted his soothsayer, who declared that the omens were unlucky and that he should wait for three times nine days. Obedient to the oracle, Nicias spent the whole period offering repeated sacrifices to appease the wrath of the gods. Meanwhile the enemy, having closed the port to him, destroyed his entire fleet. To escape by land was impossible; and neither he nor any of his men was spared by the Syracusans. When they heard of the disaster, what was the reaction of the Athenians? They were aware of Nicias' admirable steadfastness and personal courage. It never entered their heads to blame him for having accepted the decrees of providence. The only thing they reproached him for was that he had taken with him an ignorant soothsayer who had wrongly interpreted the eclipse of the moon; he should have known that, for an army in retreat, when the moon hides her face it is a favourable omen.'

From this account it is clear how strongly divination still influenced the conduct of armies and political affairs, even at the end of the century of Pericles, a period when religious belief had already been appreciably sapped by the constant attacks of the philosophers and sophists. In archaic times, in the seventh and sixth centuries, and even in the first half of the fifth, things had been very different: one has only to skim the pages of Herodotus to appreciate the almost incredible part that oracles played in the history of the Greeks and the barbarians.

*   *   *

In the *De Divinatione*, from which we have already quoted, Cicero distinguishes two kinds of prophecy: one due to art, the other to nature. He was in fact adopting Plato's distinction between *inductive* or artificial divination (*entechnos, technike*) and *intuitive* or natural divination (*atechnos, adidaktos*).

The first of these is based on the study of phenomena observed by a soothsayer; it is, as Plato says, 'the investigation of the future by means of birds and other signs'. Though it obviously rests upon irrational assumptions, the method it employs is sane and rational. The second, on the other hand, consists of a kind of madness (*mania* in Greek; *furor* in Latin) or ecstasy of divine possession. It is the kind relied upon by seers and prophetesses, Sibyls, Pythias, Bakis, who were regarded as being directly inspired by the god without perceptible intermediary; it is therefore an entirely supernatural

4

activity, theoretically and practically, as well as in its effects. For Plato, this second type was much the higher; and etymologically it is only in this case that the word *mantike* is applicable.

Nevertheless, by an extension of its meaning *mantike* came to include inductive divination, which is just as ancient as the other, having been already practised by the great 'seers' (the *manteis*) of the heroic age.

I propose to begin by describing the methods of inductive divination, leaving the question of inspired prophecy to the following chapter.

*   *   *

In their observation of natural phenomena, what must have first struck men's imagination and been accepted by them as a clear manifestation of the will of the gods, would have been marvels and prodigies. Indeed as a rule, as may be seen from the many instances to be found in the *Iliad* and the *Odyssey*, it was from prodigious events that the Homeric seers derived their predictions. I shall only mention one of these.

When the Greek chieftains were offering a sacrifice at Aulis before setting out for Troy, a serpent sprang from beneath an altar and devoured nine sparrows perched on a plane tree, eight young ones and their mother; and as soon as he had finished eating the sparrows the serpent was turned to stone. Immediately Calchas, the official augur of the army, spoke up: 'Why do you remain silent, O long-haired Achaeans? Zeus in his wisdom has sent us this great omen, predicting the tardy and remote future, an omen which will for ever be remembered. Just as the serpent has devoured these sparrows—eight fledgelings, nine including the mother—so for nine years shall we fight, and in the tenth we shall capture the great city of Troy.'

Here Cicero had no difficulty in raising 'rationalist' objections: 'Why should Calchas assume that the number of sparrows indicated the number of years, rather than of days or months? Why did he associate his prophecy with the death of these little birds, which was in no way miraculous, yet remain silent about the serpent, whose petrifaction was really marvellous? And again, what connection was there between sparrows and years?'

Criticism of this kind, however, reveals a complete mis-understanding of what, in the eyes of the ancient Greeks, constituted the essential feature of the miraculous, a feature that has been brought to light by a number of scholars, notably J. Bayet.[1] Belief in omens of this kind is to be explained by the survival of a primitive mentality that belongs to a period prior to the creation of a polytheistic and anthropomorphic mytho-logy. That extraordinary behaviour on the part of animals (who for a long time had been worshipped as gods) could determine what was to come to pass among men, was genuine magic. Thus the marvellous omen was not merely a sign of what was going to happen, essentially it was its cause; the omen and its fulfilment were fatally connected by a bond that could not be dissolved by prayer or any other religious rite. In most of the texts, however, this extremely ancient and pre-logical concep-tion is overlaid by the expression of a more recent attitude of mind.

In epic poetry it was easy for the soothsayers to discover miraculous events, which they could then simply interpret. In everyday life these were more difficult to come by, yet the soothsayers could not on this account refuse to answer the questions that were put to them. For lack of marvels they therefore usually had to be content with simple signs (*simeia*), that is to say ordinary natural phenomena, which they inter-preted as also revealing the wishes of the gods, but symbolically, by means of a conventional language whose grammar and laws were known only to themselves.

On account of their reliability and constancy, the instincts of animals were seen as a divine force. Nor must it be forgotten, moreover, that in primitive society animals had themselves been worshipped as gods long before they became mere attri-butes of the anthropomorphic gods. This was so not only in

---

[1] See his important article in *Mélanges F. Cumant* (*Ann. Inst. Phil. Hist. Or.*, IV, Brussels, 1936, pp. 27–51): 'Présages figuratifs déterminants dans l'Antiquité greco-latine'.

1. The Sanctuary of Athena Pronaia at Delphi

2. The Castelia fountain at Delphi

3. A Roman soothsayer consulting the entrails of a bull. *Detail from sculpture in the Louvre, Paris*

4. Amphora by the Andokides painter showing Apollo and Herakles struggling for the tripod, c. 530–520 B.C. *Department of Antiquities, Berlin*

Egypt, but also in Greece: the eagle of Zeus, the bear of Artemis, Apollo's wolf and Athena's owl derive from remote times when each of these animals had itself been the object of a cult. Earth and Water, the mothers shared by all living creatures, were looked upon in Greece as the primordial source of all divination: later we shall see that the Earth goddess, Gê, had occupied the prophetic sanctuary of Delphi before the coming of Apollo, and that the Pythia had to drink from the spring of Cassotis before she could foretell the future. It should be noted, however, that only very occasionally did sooth-sayers rely upon signs derived from the behaviour of terrestrial or aquatic animals.

Amongst land animals the serpent, which we have already encountered eating the sparrows in the example expounded by Calchas, appears again at the sanctuaries of Apollo and his son Asclepios (Aesculapius); at Epidaurus for example, where as we shall see that divination by incubation was practised for medical purposes. The lizard, too, had mantic qualities that were used by certain soothsayers, which is why we sometimes find it portrayed at the side of Apollo, the most prophetically gifted of all the gods, and known as *Sauroctonos*, the 'lizard-killer'. Rats, weasels and bats were also used for purposes of divination, but extremely rarely.

As for fish, they were not used for this purpose in Greece proper but only in such belatedly Hellenized countries as Syria and Lycia. We learn from Pseudo-Lucian that at Hierapolis in Syria, where there was a well-known oracle, 'a large number of sacred fish of all kinds were kept in a lake'. And in his essay, *On the Intelligence of Animals*, Plutarch says: 'I have heard it said that at Sura, a township in Lycia, people are appointed to observe fish, as we do birds in Greece, and that studying their movements as they pursue one another is regarded as a kind of art or science.' But there was nothing of this kind in Greece itself, and Plutarch was certainly expressing the opinion of the majority of his fellow countrymen when he wrote: 'Fish, being dumb, are devoid of prophetic gifts. They are con-demned to live in a place hated by the gods, where neither reason nor spiritual intelligence exists.'

In the same work however, speaking of birds, he says: 'In the art of predicting the future, the most important and most ancient part consists of bird-lore. Thanks to their speed and intelligence, and to the precision of the movements with which they respond to everything impinging upon their senses, birds are the veritable instruments of divine power. It is the gods who determine the variety of their movements, and elicit from them their cries and twitterings. Sometimes they hold them suspended in the air, sometimes they hurriedly dispatch them to hinder the acts or purposes of men or to assist in their fulfilment. This is why Euripides speaks of them as "messengers of the gods".'

This passage not only explains the prestige attaching to birds, as creatures inhabiting the sky and therefore closest to the gods like Zeus and his son Apollo (always regarded by the Greeks as being the two most inclined to reveal the future to mankind), it also draws attention to the distinctive feature of divination by birds, or ornithomancy: the observation of their flight and of their cries. The species of the bird was also important: some were 'naturally propitious', others were invariably 'of ill omen', and the significance of certain birds depended upon circumstances and the person by whom they were seen. For instance the owl, as the bird of Athena, was propitious for Athenians, but for anyone else a kind of ill omen.

Flight was especially important. In the first place, if a bird appeared to the right of someone facing north, that is to say to the east, it was a good sign; and the contrary if it appeared to the west, that is, to the left (hence the meaning of 'sinister' which originally simply meant 'left'). A bird flying high with outstretched wings was a favourable sign; one that flew low with irregular wing-beats, unfavourable. The Greeks, more subtle than the Romans, even distinguished between the various degrees of energy and poise (*hedra*) a bird displayed, though it is difficult to understand precisely how they interpreted this. Similarly, the significance of a bird's song was judged according to its volume and frequency.

All birds, particularly birds of prey, were capable of providing portents, and eventually the very word for bird (*öiños*

8

or *ornis*) came to mean 'portent'. But by a process of selection four species were above all esteemed for their prophetic significance: the eagle and vulture of Zeus, Apollo's raven and Hera's crow. However, though widely practised in Homeric and archaic times, it seems that by the classical period ornithomancy had to some extent given way to other methods of divination.

* * *

Men, free and intelligent creatures, sometimes act or speak involuntarily or unconsciously: at such moments they could be regarded as being subject to the will of the gods, like birds. 'Everything that is said,' writes Bouché-Leclercq, 'a phrase, an isolated word or exclamation, if heard by a man preoccupied with some idea unfamiliar to the man who utters it, could become for the hearer the kind of prophetic sign that the Greeks used to call a *cledon*. An unforeseen connection, a fortuitous consonance, might contain a providential warning. Presages of this kind were all the more reliable when they were uttered by those least capable of calculating their effect, by children for example.'

Cledonomancy was particularly concerned with the etymological meaning of words, especially of names, in which the Greeks always showed a marked interest. For example, as Herodotus tells us, when Leotychidas, king of Sparta, was preparing to launch the battle of Mycale, and a delegate from Samos insisted on speaking at great length, 'Leotychidas, whether hoping to hear a *cledon* or as a result of divine guidance, put this question to him: "Tell me, O guest from Samos, what is your name?" "Hegistratus", the guest replied [a name that means "army guide"]. Whereupon the Spartan, cutting him short before he could add another word, which would have destroyed the significance of the *cledon*, exclaimed: "Hegistratus! I accept the omen." And taking the name for a happy augury, he insisted upon Hegistratus remaining at his side and acting as navigator.'

In his *Life of Alexander* Plutarch tells us that the great conqueror wishing to consult Apollo about his expedition against the Persians, betook himself to Delphi. But, arriving on one of the unpropitious days when the Pythia was not allowed to speak, he sent for her, 'and when she refused to come to the temple because it was against the law, he went himself and tried to drag her there by force. Whereupon, overwhelmed by his insistence, she said: "You are invincible, my son." And immediately he heard these words, Alexander declared that it was unnecessary to consult the oracle further, since she had told him what he wished to find out.'

This belief in *cledones* was clearly related to that other belief, that words, whether lucky or unlucky, exert an intrinsic influence. At religious ceremonies, for instance, it was forbidden to 'blaspheme', that is, to utter any ill-omened word; if people could not express themselves in propitious language they must remain silent.

Some oracles would only answer those who consulted them in 'cledonistic' terms. Pausanias tells us that at Pharai, in Achaea, there was an oracle of Hermes Agoraios: 'Before the statue of the bearded Hermes was a hearth surrounded by bronze lamps. Those who wished to consult the god arrived at nightfall, burnt some incense on the hearth, and then, having filled the lamps with oil and lit them, they would place on the altar to the right of the statue a coin of local money. Only then would they approach the statue of the god and whisper in his ear the question they had come to ask, after which they would immediately leave the temple, holding their hands over their ears until they were some distance away. Then they would take their hands from their ears and the first words they heard anyone say would be the oracle's reply.'

If truth is to be found in the 'mouths of babes and sucklings' it is because they are less capable than adults of reflection. In his first epigram Callimachus describes a client's visit to Pittacos of Mytilene, one of the Seven Sages of Greece, to seek advice about choosing a wife: should he marry a girl of his own class or one wealthier and nobler than himself? Pointing to some children playing in the street with their tops Pittacos says to him: 'See them? They will teach you what you should do.' As he approached the group of children the man heard one of them call out: 'Keep in line', and at once understood this to mean that he should not marry for money. The famous *Tolle, Lege* of St Augustine's *Confessions* was uttered by a child, and was a cledonistic oracle of the same kind.

As well as unpremeditated speech, involuntary movements or shuddering might also be regarded as a presage; not only the convulsive movements of epileptics (a disease often associated with 'holiness'), but also such everyday phenomena as singing in the ears or sneezing. Since the physical act could not be voluntarily controlled it was considered reasonable to attribute it to divine influence.

There is an example of this in the *Odyssey*, towards the end of Book XVII. Penelope is sitting with her maids, longing for Odysseus to come home and drive away the suitors: 'As she finished speaking, Telemachus sneezed so loudly that the noise echoed through the house. Penelope turned to Eumaeus with a smile, and said: "Find this stranger and bring him to me. Did you not hear how my son sneezed a blessing on what I was saying? Surely, this means death for every one of the suitors." ' Or again, there is Plutarch's story of how before the battle of Salamis Themistocles was offering up a sacrifice beside the admiral's ship, when three young Persian prisoners of war were brought to him. 'As the sacrificial flame rose high and clear above the altar, the seer Euphrantides caught sight of them and, at the same moment someone on the right of the crowd sneezed. Recognizing it as a sign, the seer at once took Themistocles by the hand and ordered him to consecrate the prisoners and sacrifice them to Dionysus Omestes. "Thus", said he, "shall the safety and victory of the Greeks be assured." ' Reluctantly Themistocles had to do so. In *Anabasis* Xenophon provides yet another example. One day, as he was concluding a speech to the Ten Thousand, someone began sneezing, and 'at this sound all the soldiers knelt down as one man in honour of the god.'

In this case the sneezing was looked upon as a sign of heavenly approval of the speaker's words; in the previous one it was the fact that the sneeze came from the right that proved it to be a propitious sign.

*   *   *

Hieromancy, or divination by examining the entrails of sacrificial animals, seems to have been introduced into Greece from Etruria, but it became extremely popular in the classical period. 'There was a time,' says Alain, 'when men were guided in their undertakings by the flight of birds; they knew where to find water and pasture by examining the stomachs of the deer they killed, and from the contents of birds' crops they learnt to distinguish which grains were safe for them to eat. It was this that gave rise to the political custom of deciding important questions by observing the entrails of animals.'

Whatever the origin of hieromancy, and it remains in dispute, its principles appear to have been much more complex than those of ornithomancy. The latter depended on the belief that the movements of birds were dictated by Providence: the latter meant accepting not only that somehow the gods had marked the animals' entrails with the signs they wished to convey to men, but also that the priest was divinely inspired to select for sacrifice the particular animal that could provide the appropriate answer. But as we have already seen with regard to the interpretation of prodigies, objections of this kind present no serious obstacles to faith.

Since sacrifice was always the supreme religious act in Greece there was never any lack of victims, and hieromancy was practised on all kinds of animals, but especially goats, lambs and calves. Similarly, though all the entrails could furnish useful information, the liver was of particular importance; the three main points to be examined being the lobes, the gall-duct and the artery. Thus in Euripides' *Electra*, before killing Aegisthus, Orestes helps him perform a sacrifice from which it becomes clear that a murder is imminent. As Aegisthus takes the sacred entrails from Orestes to examine them he discovers that one lobe of the liver is missing, and the blood-vessels near the gall-duct reveal disquieting protrusions. His expression immediately betrays his dismay and Orestes asks him what it is that is troubling him. 'Stranger,' Aegisthus replies, 'I fear a trap has been set for me. I have a mortal enemy, the son of Agamemnon, and he is at war with all my house.'

The missing part of the liver, whose absence was of such

dire significance, was called by the Roman haruspices *caput jecoris*, the 'head of the liver'. Its atrophy or destruction was always regarded as the most unmistakable sign, a sure presage of ruin or death; and it was in this way that not only Aegisthus but historical figures like Cimon, Agesilaus and Alexander the Great received warning of their approaching end.

The importance of the liver for purposes of divination had two notable consequences. It led to an early development of anatomical knowledge of this organ; and it also directly influenced the theories of Plato and Aristotle with regard to inspired divination, as well as, in a more general way, their notions of physiology.

Closely connected with hieromancy was the art of divination by fire, or pyromancy. In Homeric times, when hieromancy was as yet unknown, in order to find out if their victims were acceptable to the gods the priests would first cut off the thighs and burn them on the altar, observing the brightness of the flame, the appearance of the smoke, and how soon the flesh burnt and shrivelled. In the passage from the *Life of Themistocles* quoted above the seer regarded it as noteworthy that the altar flame 'rose high and clear above the victims'.

In classical times the examination of the entrails was normally followed by the complete or partial burning of the victim. At Olympia they were boiled in a cauldron, as witness this prodigy described by Herodotus: 'The following miraculous adventure happened to Hippocrates, the father of Peisistratus, when he was taking part in the festival of Olympia as a private citizen. He had sacrificed the customary animals, and the cauldrons, filled with flesh and water, had been made ready, when suddenly, before the fire had been lit, they started to boil and overflow. Chilon of Sparta (one of the Seven Sages), who chanced to be present and saw this miracle, warned Hippocrates that he should not have a child. But Hippocrates paid no heed to him, and eventually Peisistratus was born to him, who became tyrant of Athens.'

There was also a form of vegetable pyromancy which was encouraged by the Pythagoreans in preference to animal sacrifices because they disapproved of any shedding of blood. At

Delphi, for example, the smoke of the incense and the crackling of the laurel-wood and barley in the flames were observed by the priests.

* * *

The variety of inanimate objects used in divination was almost unlimited. Here I shall only refer to the use of water, mirrors and trees. In the eyes of the Greeks water, though not the fish that live in it, possessed important supernatural virtues. Springs and rivers were regarded as divinities, usually beneficent and gifted with infallible clairvoyance. In Homer, the Olympians swore by the waters of the Styx as a most sacred oath. And, as we shall see, the water drunk by the prophets was a powerful source of inspiration. But inductive divination also made use of hydromancy.

In Syria, in the impressive circus of Afka at the source of the Nahr Ibrahim (the ancient river Adonis), the spot where Maurice Barrès professed to have heard 'the crazed howling of the mourners' weeping the death of Adonis, there was a temple of Aphrodite, the goddess who fell in love with a mortal. 'Near the temple,' says Zosimus, 'was a pool. Those who came to worship Aphrodite brought presents of gold and silver, of fine linen and other precious materials, and if their gifts were acceptable to the goddess, the woven cloth as well as the solid objects sank to the bottom. But if on the contrary she rejected them, the stuffs and even the objects made of gold or silver or other heavy material were seen to float naturally on the surface of the pool.' It is said that it was in this way that the people of Palmyra received warning of the approaching collapse of their power.

Pausanias tell us that in the sanctuary of Demeter at Patras there was a spring that was an infallible oracle for the sick who came to consult the goddess: 'A mirror was attached to a string and then lowered, so that it just skimmed the surface of the water without actually penetrating it. Then, having prayed to Demeter and burnt incense, they looked into the mirror.' Here, the mirror seems to have been only an accessory, used to reveal the magic properties of the water.

According to André Delatte there were, strictly speaking, two kinds of divination by mirrors, or catoptromancy. 'The one made no appeal to any supernatural power, but relied upon the more or less magical property of any glittering surface to encourage divination by exciting the imagination. To this type belongs the method parodied by Aristophanes in *The Acharnians*, when Lamachos says to his slave "Here you, pour some oil on this shield. I can see on the bronze an old man who will be tried for cowardice." The other kind of catoptromancy had a very clear religious character, and employed invocations to both gods and demons. In later times this was to enjoy far greater success than the former.'[1]

The Earth, as I have already said, was, like water, a primordial source of revelation, and divination by trees was undoubtedly connected with the Earth cult, since she was the mother of vegetation as well as of mankind. At Delphi, where before the coming of Apollo the Earth had been 'the first prophetess', a bronze tree was erected near her statue. But when we speak of divination by trees it is to the prophetic oaks of Dodona that our thoughts first turn.

This oracle, which was known to Homer, was looked upon as the most ancient in Greece. In Epirus, a cold, windswept country at the foot of mount Tomaros, ravaged by storms, the Pelagians, ancestors of the Greeks, believed that the voice of Zeus could be heard in the murmuring of the oak trees stirred by the wind. Associated with Zeus was Dione, identified with the Earth goddess. Her priestesses, the Peleiades, and the priests of Zeus, the Selle, were the attendants of the oracle. In the *Iliad* the Selle are described by two epithets that signify that they slept on the ground and never washed their feet. According to one writer, 'at Dodona there was an oak consecrated to Zeus, in which oak was an oracle whose wives (the Peleiades) were prophetesses. When those who came to consult the oracle approached the oak, its branches trembled for a moment and then the women's voices could be heard, saying: "Zeus declares this or that." '

---

[1] *La catoptromancie grecque et ses dérivés* (Bibl. Univ. de Liège, Monograph No. 48, 1932).

This brief account can scarcely satisfy our curiosity. How, for instance, did the Peleiades interpret the rustling of the foliage? Since Plato when speaking in his *Phaedrus* of prophetic ecstasy treats the 'priestesses of Dodona' on an equal footing with the Delphic Pythia, it would seem probable that when interpreting the sounds of the tree they were inspired and in this sense combined both intuitive and inductive divination. Yet as with all the great oracles of Greece different methods were employed at Dodona successively, and even simultaneously. We know that the Selle foretold the future by interpreting the sound of bronze, since Callimachus speaks of them as 'servants of the bowl which is never silent'. On this point there are various traditions. Some writers speak of there being several bronze bowls suspended side by side, so that when one of them blown by the wind banged against another the sound produced was prolonged indefinitely. We also find references to a more perfect instrument that was used by the Corcyreans: a bronze bowl and the statue of a child holding a whip, which consisted of three bronze chains with metal studs, stood side by side on two pillars; and when the wind blew the chains, these struck the bowl.

Both these methods of divination, 'by bronze' and 'by trees', were alike in as much as both depended upon sounds caused by the play of the wind, the attendants of the oracle hearing the voice of Zeus either in the rustling of the leaves or in the ringing of the bronze. At a later period there was another and very different type of divination which is referred to by Cicero: divination by lot, or cleromancy.

The famous excavations of Carapanos in the last century and those carried out more recently at Dodona yielded amongst other things a large number of sheets of lead, which were used by clients of the oracle: they would inscribe them with the questions they wished to ask, and then hand them to the priests. Some of these record public enquiries undertaken on behalf of cities. On one of them, for example, the people of Corcyra 'ask Zeus Naios and Dione to which gods and heroes it behoves them to offer prayers and sacrifice if we are to avoid civil strife'. At Delphi and a number of other sanctuaries we

shall later come across other examples of this kind of purely
theological consultation, which scarcely called for any prophetic
skill on the part of the oracle. But the majority of the questions
are concerned with such purely private and commonplace
matters as how to maintain or restore the health of the clients
or of their relations, or how to succeed in business. One of
these seems to be almost pointless: 'Agis asks Zeus Naios and
Dione whether he lost the blankets and pillows himself or
whether they were stolen by someone outside the household.'
Another is much more serious: 'Lysanias asks Zeus and Dione
whether the child which Nyla is carrying is really his.'

Sometimes the god's answer is inscribed above the question,
but on the tablets that have so far been recovered the reply is
almost invariably illegible. From one of them, however, it is
clear that the god had advised a man who was hesitating about
the choice of a career to follow that of his father, a fisherman.[1]

*   *   *

Cleromancy was practised not only at Dodona but at the
majority of the oracles in Greece; even, as we shall see, at
Delphi. The reason for this is more easily understood when
we realize that in the opinion of the ancients the drawing of
lots was governed, not by chance, but by the will of the gods.
In Book VII of the *Iliad* lots are drawn to decide which of the
Achaean chieftains shall accept Hector's challenge, and the
Achaeans beseech the gods to choose the best man. At Athens,
and doubtless in other cities as well, the majority of magistrates
and judges were chosen by lot; and a number of machines
designed for this purpose (the *cleroteria* referred to by Aristotle
in his *Constitution of Athens*) have been found. So widespread
was the practice of cleromancy that it gave rise to certain
words which later were to take on the more general sense of
'prophesying'. For example, the verb *anaireo*, constantly used
when speaking of the answers given by the Pythia, originally
meant simply 'to draw lots'. Dice, knuckle-bones and beans

[1] With regard to Dodona, see the new oracular texts published in *Bulletin de Corr. hell.*, 83 (1959), pp. 669–73.

were all used for drawing lots, while in Attica, at the sanctuary
of Skiron dedicated to Athena Skiras, the oracle employed dice.

Atmospheric phenomena, *meteora*, were obviously signs of
the will of the gods; especially of Zeus, the god of the atmosphere and the sky. The weightiest presage of all, the one that
could negate or confirm all others, was thunder. In the *Iliad*,
whenever Zeus wishes to encourage one of the Greek or Trojan heroes he does so by hurling a thunderbolt to the right of
him. Rain also comes from Zeus, and was regarded as a sign
of his will, a *diosemeion*. But beyond the clouds and all other
atmospheric phenomena were the stars. Astrology reached
Greece from outside, from the Orient. Yet though its complicated laws and inexorable fatalism scarcely seem to be in
harmony with their genius, there were two things that pre-
disposed the Greeks to accept it. In the first place, at a very
early period, they had a number of superstitions connected with
the stars: in Homer, Sirius, 'Orion's Dog', was a star of ill-
omen; the Spartans would never embark on a campaign before
the full moon, which appears to be the reason why they did
not arrive at Marathon until the battle was over. And, in the
second place, astrology is closely related to astrolatry, the
religious worship of the stars as gods. Now there was a whole
current of Greek thought, deriving from the East and extend-
ing through the Pythagoreans as far as Plato, which readily
accepted this astral mysticism and looked upon celestial bodies
as the most primitive of the gods to have been worshipped by
mankind. Yet it was only with the victories of Alexander that
the beliefs of the Chaldeans made a really profound impact upon
Greece.

The underlying principle of astrology is that the universe
comprises a single organism, all the parts of which are closely
interrelated, and that man, this microcosm, is continually
exposed to influences emanating from the whole universe, the
cosmos, whose course is determined by that of the stars. It
was this that made horoscopes so important, since they
depended upon being able to determine the precise point of the
zodiac which was visibly above the horizon at the moment of
a man's birth. Cumont maintains that 'before the coming of

Christianity the only opponents of astrology were those who denied any possibility of knowledge, that is to say radical sceptics and neo-academics like Carneades. At the court of Severus, in the third century A.D., anyone who attempted to deny the influence of the planets on human affairs would have been regarded as being even more unreasonable than we should consider a man who believed in it.' And, indeed, as everybody knows, our language still bears traces of a belief in astrology in such words as *lunatic* and *saturnine*.[1]

*   *   *

At this point it might be appropriate to recall such famous Greek seers as Calchas, or Amphiaraos the prophet-king, or Tiresias, the blind old man whose story is so closely linked with that of Oedipus. But all these were legendary figures. Of those known to history, it is enough to mention Megistias of Acarnania of whom Herodotus speaks; one of the little group of determined men who, under the leadership of Leonidas, awaited the arrival of the Persians at Thermopylae in 480 B.C. When the barbarians had surrounded the pass, 'Megistias, having inspected the sacrificial victim, announced to the Greeks the death that awaited them at dawn.' Whereupon Leonidas sent away all the allied troops and Megistias with them, 'lest they, too, should perish'. But the seer, having dismissed his only son who was serving with the army, himself refused to leave and perished at his post. The poet Simonides wrote this epitaph for him and had it engraved upon his tomb:

'Beneath this monument lies the illustrious Megistias, who fell beneath the blows of the Medes on the banks of the Sperchios. As a prophet he had clearly foreseen the fate that awaited him, but he refused to abandon the Spartan chieftains'.

[1] The question of astrology has been admirably treated by F. Cumont in the following works: *Astrology and Religion among the Greeks and Romans*, New York, 1912; *Les religions orientales dans le paganisme romain; L'Egypte des astrologues*, Brussels, 1937.

2

INSPIRED DIVINATION

Purely inductive methods of divination were clearly far from perfect. Except in the case of prodigies, and they by definition are infrequent, it was not always easy to be sure which signs were divinely inspired. Moreover, in the interpretation of signs there was always the chance of error, and sometimes two soothsayers would produce different versions. In Rome, Cato was to wonder how two haruspices could look at one another without laughing, and even in the *Iliad* some of the heroes display a certain scepticism with regard to prophecies. Aristophanes in *The Knights* and *The Birds*, and the tragic poets in several plays, make fun of the whole tribe of soothsayers, whom they accuse of greed and duplicity. When Euripides says 'the good prophet is a man skilled in conjecture,' he is implying that inductive divination depends less upon revelations from on high than upon the resources of an astute and subtle mind.

In principle, then, how much safer was divination that was directly inspired by a god and independent of any material signs. This was genuine *mantike*, in the original sense of the word (*mania*: madness), caused by possession, by the literal presence of the god in the soul of the prophet or prophetess, who thus received the revelation direct from heaven. This superior form of divination appears already, though rather hesitantly, in Homer. In Book VII of the *Iliad* the Trojan seer, Helenus, 'suddenly knows in his heart what the gods are planning'. In Book XI of the *Odyssey* Tiresias prophesies quite independently of any sign; and in Book XV Helen is suddenly inspired with the gift of prophecy: 'Listen to me. These words come to me from the gods and they will surely come to pass.' Finally, in Book XX, the soothsayer Theoclymenus foretells the death of the suitors: 'I see the walls splashed with blood. The porch is filled with ghosts. So is the court—ghosts hurrying to darkness and to hell. The sun dies in the heavens and a deathly cloud hangs over everything.'

Dreams, too, play an important part in epic poetry, and their capricious and mysterious nature encourages belief in oneiromancy. We have seen that any involuntary word, thought or deed might be regarded as a supernatural sign. And what could be more involuntary, more unconscious, than dreams, which occur when both will and consciousness are overcome by sleep? Thus oneiromancy, the interpretation of dreams, is to be found in all ages and in every country. All pagan peoples believed in it, as well as the Jews, as may be seen from the story of Joseph interpreting dreams at the court of Pharaoh.

Homer was aware that dreams are ambiguous and that it was not easy to distinguish between reliable ones, which reach us 'through the gate of horn', and misleading ones that come 'through the gate of ivory'. Besides, dreams might include every kind of prodigy and presage enumerated in the previous chapter (the dreamer might even see the entrails of a sacrificial animal), in short all those signs that, in the waking state, were known to be useful for purposes of divination. Thus a good interpreter of dreams had to be a master of the whole science of divination; and indeed the interpretation of dreams gave rise to a voluminous and complex body of doctrine which is known to us from the compilation made by Artemidorus of Ephesus in the Roman epoch.

In popular belief, frightening or obscene dreams, nightmares, were produced by malicious nocturnal spirits. Thus the followers of Pythagoras sought to calm their minds before sleeping by eating a frugal supper (in particular they eschewed beans and meat), as well as by prayer and music, hoping in this way to protect themselves from demonic visitations (the Catholic office of Compline still retains the words *procul recedant somnia et noctium phantasmata*) and to encourage the true dreams inspired by the gods. Plato makes the same point in Book IX of *The Republic*: in accordance with his tripartite division of the soul, he says, one should seek to curb those parts of it responsible for desire and anger, and to stimulate the third, the dwelling-place of wisdom, if one wishes to learn the truth from dreams.

Thus both the Pythagoreans and the Platonists prepared themselves for sleep by ascetic practices; and, as we shall see, the same thing was done in the sanctuaries of Asclepios with a view to healing the sick. Aristotle wrote a most curious treatise, *On Divination Through Dreams*, in which many of the observations he records agree with the findings of modern psychologists. He is especially concerned with the clinical significance of dreams, to which many physicians today attach great importance.

The outstanding god of medicine was the son of the prophet-god Apollo, Asclepios, known to the Romans as Aesculapius. The most famous of his sanctuaries were those at Epidaurus, Cos and Pergamon. In the second century of our era, the fame of the last of these was to be spread by the orator Aelius Aristides who, believing himself to be suffering from innumerable diseases and being by nature religious and even superstitious, was one of Asclepios' 'model patients'.[1]

At Epidaurus in Argolis, at the foot of the hill on which stands the most beautiful of all Greek theatres, may be seen the ruins of the god's sanctuary which, in addition to the customary buildings—vestibule, temple, altar and gymnasium—contained two more unusual ones: a mysterious round monument or *tholos*, and the remains of a vast two-storeyed hall which served as a dormitory for the sick; and which the inscription refers to both as *enkoimetrion* (the place of incubation) or *abaton* (the holy and secret place). It was here that the invalids, having performed the preliminary rites, came to spend the night on beds made of animal hides, hoping that as they slept Asclepios would grant them an instantaneous and miraculous cure; that is to say, a dream that would reveal to them the appropriate treatment for their illness and the regime to be followed.

The preliminary rites were extensive. In particular the patients had to drink from a spring of salt water and bathe themselves; in this respect Epidaurus reminds one of a modern

[1] See A. Boulanger, *Aelius Aristide,* Paris, 1913.

5. Detail of the amphora showing Apollo and Herakles struggling for the tripod

6. Vase depicting the contest of Herakles and Apollo for the tripod. *British Museum*

7. Amphora. Preparations for sacrifice and dedication of tripods. *British Museum*

8. Didymeion. A general view of excavations made by the German archaeologists

spa. But they also had to offer a sacrifice, undergo various forms of abstinence and fasting and take part in religious ceremonies at all hours of the day and night; all of which no doubt helped to create in many of them a sense of expectation that would reach its climax during the night they spent in the holy hall. It would appear that the visitations of Asclepios did not usually occur during profound sleep but when the patients were in a semi-waking state; and then in the form of hypnotic hallucinations.[1] It is also probable that the priests, both before and after the night of consecration, prescribed various treatments or elaborated those recommended by the god, drawing upon their practical experience and at least the rudiments of medical knowledge.

When they were cured the patients showed their gratitude to the god by presenting him with votive gifts representing the limb or organ that had been the cause of their suffering. As to the stelae describing these miraculous cures, that were found during the excavations of Epidaurus, they were doubtless inspired by the priests, who would have been quick to appreciate their advertising value. Amongst these accounts we may read the story of a child, dumb from birth, who suddenly began to speak, or that of a man with hideous blotches on his forehead: 'Pandarus the Thessalian, being asleep, had this vision. It seemed to him that the god covered the blotches with a bandage and instructed him that as soon as he left the dormitory he was to remove it and present it to the sanctuary as an offering. At day-break, as soon as he got up he took off the bandage and, perceiving that his face was now free of blemish, he dedicated it to the sanctuary.' Or again there is the charming tale of Euphanes, a child from Epidaurus: 'Suffering from the stone, he fell asleep. It seemed to him that the god appeared and said to him: "What will you give me if I cure you?" "Ten knuckle-bones," replied the child. Whereupon the god burst out laughing and promised he should be healed. And in the morning he was.'

---

[1] The question of hypnotic hallucinations and the technique of 'incubation' have been interestingly treated in an article by A. Taffin, 'On rêvait dans les temples d'Esculape'. (Bull. de l'Ass. G.-Budé, 1960, pp. 325–66).

During the Hellenistic and Roman epochs, the sanctuaries of Serapis attracted a great part of the devotees of Asclepios, and cures were effected in the same way, through oneiromancy. At Oropos, near the frontier between Attica and Boeotia, a temple was founded in honour of the prophet-king Amphiaraos, and the ruins of this Amphiareion have now been excavated. Here, the clients of the oracle had first of all to abstain from drinking wine for three days and fast for twenty-four hours, then, having sacrificed a ram and skinned it, they spent the night in the sacred precinct, sleeping on the sheepskin and awaiting the beneficent vision.

Quite different, and very unusual, was the mantic procedure employed in the cave of Trophonios, at Lebedea in Boeotia. Trophonios was an ancient divinity, demoted to the rank of hero, who according to tradition had helped his brother Agamedes to build the first temple at Delphi. His oracle consisted of a grotto, or rather a deep chasm opening into the side of the mountain. According to Pausanias, this opening was just wide enough to admit a human body. The petitioner who was bold enough to brave the terrors of a subterranean journey had first of all to offer a number of sacrifices, especially a black ram whose entrails were then inspected by the priests in order to find out whether or not Trophonios was prepared to grant an interview. If he was, the patient was conducted by two boys to the stream Herkyna, where he bathed and anointed himself with oil; after which he had to drink from the fountains of Lethe (Forgetfulness) and Mnemosyne (Memory). He then climbed down a ladder to the entrance of the chasm and, holding a honey-cake in each hand to appease the infernal powers, inserted his legs into the opening. Immediately he was as it were snatched away to the deepest part of the cave, the *adyton*, where he was supposed to receive Trophonios' revelation in a vision. Later, completely dazed and in very poor shape, he was brought back feet foremost by the same route, placed in the seat of Mnemosyne and questioned by the priests about the impressions he had received, which had to be inscribed on a tablet.

Amphiaraos and Trophonios were mythical figures, but in

the same way that the dying were inspired with the gift of prophecy (in the *Iliad* Patroclus foretells the fate of Hector who has defeated him, as Hector does for Achilles at the moment when he is about to strike the fatal blow), so the dead, especially those who were made heroes on account of their courage or holiness, were able to foresee and reveal the future, as Tiresias does to Odysseus in the *Odyssey*. Necromancy consisted in the power to evoke the ghosts of the dead in order to question them; as the Faithful do in Aeschylus' *Persae*, when they interrogate the shade of king Darius.

A curious inscription from Roman times makes it clear that, even as late as this, the tomb of a priestess might become an oracle, at least for a restricted circle of initiates, or *mystes*. Here is the text of this epitaph, which was found at Thyatira in Lydia: 'To the memory of Ammias, priestess of the gods, her children, the disciples of the gods, dedicate this altar and funerary urn. Let him who would learn from me the truth pray before this altar, and whatever he may ask of me I will impart to him, whether in daylight or in darkness.'[1]

* * *

Dreams, the oracle of Trophonios, necromancy, all these belong to the nocturnal aspect of intuitive divination. The inspiration of prophets and prophetesses represents its daylight side, for their powers of prediction were independent of darkness and infernal visions. Does this mean, then, that they were fully conscious? Hardly, for when they were possessed they were in a state of ecstasy or delirium which has sometimes been attributed to hypnosis. Amongst the methods of inspired divination we may include those that were practised in the most remote regions of Greece, in Syria at Heliopolis (Baalbek) and Hierapolis (Bambyce), as well as in Africa by the oracle of Ammon in the Libyan desert (the oasis of Siwah).

At Heliopolis, we learn from Macrobius, 'the gold statue of the god is borne on a litter by the notabilities of the district, whose heads are shaven and who have purified themselves by

[1] This epitaph was published by L. Robert in his *Etudes anatoliennes*, pp. 129–33, Paris, 1937.

prolonged continence. They are imbued with a divine spirit and they go not where they choose but where they are driven by the god.' At Hierapolis, according to Pseudo-Lucian, 'the Syrian Apollo moves by himself and delivers his oracles himself in the following manner. When he wishes to speak he [obviously he means the statue] begins to stir on his throne. Whereupon the priests at once lift him down, for if they fail to do so he becomes more and more agitated and starts sweating. Then, as they bear him on their shoulders, he makes them change direction and carry him from place to place. Presently the high priest appears and addresses all kinds of questions to him. If the god disapproves he withdraws; if he approves, he makes his bearers move forward, as though he were driving them with reins. It is in this manner that they receive his oracles, without which no action, either religious or political, is undertaken.'

At the oasis of Ammon in Libya, where the oracle enjoyed such a reputation amongst the Greeks that Alexander the Great insisted upon consulting it, the statue of the god was an almost shapeless idol, a simple *xoanon*. It is thus described by Diodorus Siculus: 'The idol of the god Ammon is covered with emeralds and other jewels and it delivers its oracles in the most unusual way. It is borne on a long golden barge by twenty-four priests, who support it on their shoulders, moving automatically as though they are urged on by the god's will. And they are followed by a procession of girls and women singing a succession of pæans and hymns as they go.' René Vallois has suggested the following rationalist explanation 'When one comes to think about it, it would appear that the method here described was probably regarded by the seers as being the most perfect, and it is easy to understand why the Greeks continued to believe in the prophecies of Ammon even when they had lost faith in other oracles. Remember how easily, in the last century, people believed in table-turning: if without realizing it a group of people co-ordinate their movements, only the slightest effort is necessary on the part of each individual. This is the explanation of the twenty-four priests referred to by Diodorus; and the singing of the women, by inducing a state of semi-consciousness, would facilitate the illusion. For the onlookers, who knew nothing of the psychological phenomenon discovered by the experiments of Faraday and Chevreuil, the number of them involved would seem to exclude any intervention of human will.'[1]

*   *   *

In Greece itself, in Asia Minor and Greater Greece, and in Southern Italy, there was a tradition of isolated prophets and, more especially, prophetesses. Here, indeed, women assume a much greater importance than they had in the sphere of inductive divination, which relied upon the interpretation of signs. With regard to intuitive, inspired divination the female spirit seems to have been more receptive to divine influence and better suited to serve as *medium*.

The Sibyls, far more renowned than the male prophets known as Bakis, are lost in the mists of remotest time. At Delphi itself the 'rock of the Sibyl' preserved the memory of Herophila who was supposed to have been prophesying in the time of the earliest Pythias. Also well known were the Sibyls of Erythraea, of whom the philosopher Heracleitus of Ephesus speaks most respectfully, and of Cumae. In the Roman period twelve Sibyls have been enumerated.

It seems to me probable that the earliest of these legendary figures was born at the time of the great religious movement that took place around the eighth century B.C., a movement whose mystical character was favourable to a belief in intuitive divination directly inspired by a god, most frequently by Apollo. Almost certainly the Dionysian mysteries owe their origin to the same movement, for, as we shall see, Dionysus was almost as much revered at Delphi as Apollo himself.

The prototype of the Sibyls, who occur in both epic and dramatic poetry, was the strange figure of the young Trojan woman, Cassandra, the daughter of Priam and beloved of Apollo. In the hope of seducing her, the god had granted her the power of prophecy, but when she rejected his love he

[1] R. Vallois, 'L'oracle libyen et Alexandre', in the *Revue des études grecques*, 44 (1931), pp. 121–52.

decreed that no one should believe her. Thus it was useless for her to warn the Trojans of the terrible misfortunes in store for them, or to urge them not to admit the wooden horse. After the fall of Troy the king of Mycenae took her aboard his ship as his prisoner and concubine; and in his *Agamemnon* Aeschylus portrays Cassandra's prophetic madness, a madness that affects her almost like a physical illness, the attacks being interspersed with periods of sanity. We see her writhing in the power of the god who, having deprived her of reason, reveals to her crazed mind terrifying visions of the crime that is about to be committed: Agamemnon, struck down in his own bathhouse by his wife Clytemnestra and 'bleeding like a stuck pig'. Then she goes on to predict that she herself will soon be the second victim: 'This palace stinks of murder and spilt blood . . . the air is foul with graveyard exhalations.'

Just as Zeus had issued his oracles at the temple of Dodona (see above pp. 15–16), so towards the seventh century Apolline divination was established as a kind of 'mantic institution' in the sanctuaries dedicated to this son of Zeus, who out of benevolence towards mankind made known to them his father's will.

The sceptical Lucian enumerates the principal oracular shrines of Apollo in an entertaining passage in which Zeus is supposed to be speaking. The 'father of the gods and of mankind', as Homer calls him, is humorously complaining that the Olympians are far from enjoying perfect happiness, despite what poets and philosophers say about them; for example, the author of the *Iliad*, 'that blind old man who insists upon our happiness and describes everything that goes on in heaven although he couldn't even see what was happening on earth!' Men are continually worrying the gods with their affairs: 'Look at Apollo, for instance, who has taken on the difficult job of prophesying and, as a result, is almost plagued to death by the continual demand for oracles. One minute he has to be at Delphi, the next at Colophon or Xanthos; then he has to dash off to Claros or Delos or Branchidae. Anywhere, in fact, where the priestess, having drunk the holy water and chewed the laurel leaves, begins writhing on her tripod and calling upon him to appear, he must be ready to turn up without an instant's delay and start spinning out oracles; otherwise he would disgrace the whole profession!'

Despite what Lucian says, however, which implies that all the oracles of Apollo employed the services of a priestess as at Delphi, at Claros it was a man who was responsible. M. Louis Robert, who recently excavated the temple of Apollo at Claros[1] writes: 'The peculiarity of this splendid temple was the *adyton*, the place of mystery, inaccessible to the uninitiated, where the oracles were pronounced. From several texts we know that the type of divination practised at Claros was by water, and that the priest could only prophesy when he had drunk the water from a mysterious spring, for which he had to "descend into a grotto"; we know also that there were "caverns" and an "underground chamber". To me it seems clear that all these texts refer to an artificial cavern constructed beneath the temple. . . . In addition, the oracle functioned at night: we have to imagine the scene taking place in darkness, lit only by torches or lamps. . . . Excavation discovered this *adyton* in a state of unhoped-for preservation, and the plan of this setting for the oracle is unique. In the *pronaos*, 40 feet from the façade, two stairways descend, one to the north, the other to the south. . . . Each of these leads down by four high steps into a gallery, both of which join to form a single corridor running towards the centre of the temple. . . . In the course of some 30 yards this passage, which is scarcely more than 5 feet 6 inches high by 2 feet 2 inches wide, changes direction seven times at right-angles. . . . The first, vaulted, chamber to which one thus gains access was a waiting-room for the priests who, as we know from inscriptions, included, in addition to the prophet of the year, the priest of Apollo appointed for life, the thespiod, also a life appointment, who was responsible for putting the oracles into verse, and one or two secretaries. This

[1] A full account of Robert's discoveries at Claros will be found in a lecture he gave in 1953 at the University of Ankara: 'Les fouilles de Claros', published in the *Annuaire du Collège de France*, 1957–9, and in *Türk Arkeloit Dergisi*, 1957–9. See also the *American Journal of Archaeology*, 63 (1959), pp. 83–4; and 64 (1960), p. 66. In this last volume there is a photograph of the first room of the *adyton*, with the omphalos, (Fig. 10, pl. 13).

first room held an astonishing surprise for us: (the sacred stone of Apollo, the *omphalos*, was lying in the northern part of the room, an oval stone of blue marble, 26½ inches high. .). Thus Claros too had its *omphalos*, like Delphi, and it was kept in the outer room reserved for the priesthood. . . . From here a tunnel, some 3 yards in length, where one could only walk by stooping, led to the second room, also vaulted and much narrower. At the entrance was a slightly raised step, and the entrance could be closed by a door or curtain. Through this, apparently, only the prophet would pass, disappearing into the subterranean darkness and obscurity on his way to the last and most mysterious chamber and the secret well. We found this well: but Pliny the Elder was mistaken in describing it as noxious, for the water turned out to be quite drinkable.'

The sanctuary of the Branchidae, known as the Didymeion, was situated on land belonging to the great city of Miletus.[1] The legendary founder of the oracle was Branchos, and the temple was cared for by his descendants, the Branchidae. From the excavation of the Didymeion carried out by the Germans it is possible to reconstruct the way in which consultation of the oracle was effected. First of all clients went to a building known as the *chresmographeion*, or office; then, at a given time on the appointed day, they presented themselves at the entrance to the temple. From here two lateral doors led to the underground *adyton*, 14 feet below the level of the temple. As at Claros, both doors opened into vaulted passages leading to the prophetic chamber. The clients remained in the room opening off the *adyton*. The seer and his attendants continued to the bottom of the underground chamber by the other passage; and all the clients could see of him was as he passed along the sacred way towards the waters of the spring. There, having been shut up perhaps for several days, the prophetess awaited them, ready to receive and pronounce the thoughts of the god. Once the ceremony was concluded, the clients retraced their steps, left the temple and returned to the *chresmographeion*. Then, after an official report had been made out

[1] For the oracle of the Didymeion see the article by B. Haussoulier, in the *Revue de philologie*, 44 (1920), pp. 268–77.

and the god's answer been translated into solemn words, usually in verse, copies of it were handed to the clients.

There is a very interesting passage in Herodotus where he describes a consultation at the Didymeion. The Lydian Pactyes, who had led a revolt of his countrymen against the Persians and been defeated, took refuge at Kyme in Aeolis, and Cyrus, the Persian king, demanded that he should be handed over to him. 'The people of Kyme sent representatives to Branchidae to enquire how they should behave towards Pactyes without offending the gods. The oracle's answer was that they should surrender Pactyes to the Persians, and when this was reported to the Kymeans they were disposed to do so. But though the majority of them were of this opinion, Aristodicos, son of Heracleides, either because he distrusted the oracle or because he thought that the delegates had not spoken the truth, persuaded the Kymeans to wait until fresh delegates, of whom he should be one, had had time to interrogate the god a second time with regard to Pactyes. This time Aristodicos himself put the question to the god, who gave the same answer as before. Whereupon Aristodicos deliberately walked around the temple, driving away all the sparrows and other birds that were nesting there. While he was thus occupied, it seems, a voice from within the sanctuary spoke to him, saying: "Most impious of men, how dare you do what you are doing? Driving away the suppliants from my temple?" Without losing countenance, Aristodicos answered: "O mighty Lord, since thou so helpest thy suppliants, why dost thou still command the people of Kyme to surrender theirs?" To which the god replied: "I order them to do so as the price of your impiety that you may the sooner be destroyed. Thus you will learn that it is not seemly to ask the oracle whether it is right to betray those who seek favours of you." When these words were reported to the Kymean people, they were unwilling to risk either being destroyed for surrendering Pactyes to the Persians or being besieged for refusing to do so and they therefore sent him away out of their country, to Mytilene.'

Commenting on this tale in his *Histoire des Oracles*, Fontenelle remarks: 'It seems clear from his insulting words that the god was extremely annoyed, but it seems equally clear that Aristodicos was by no means convinced that it was a god who pronounced the oracle, since he sought to confuse him by the comparison with the sparrows; and when he succeeded in doing so, he was even less likely to accept him as a god.' It is quite true that such an off-hand attitude towards oracles was by no means rare in Greece, though curiously enough it went hand in hand with complete faith in, and obedience to, divine commands.

In any case, we are not obliged to accept the historical truth of this story. Roland Crahay regards it as being a specimen of 'the kind of apologetic literature that was put out by the sanctuaries; a parable to warn people that if they put immoral questions to the oracle they would be condemned and punished',[1] for a proper respect on the part of those who approached the gods was one of the most sacred principles of Greek religion.

In addition to Delphi, Claros and Branchidae, Lucian also mentions in the same passage a number of other prophetic sanctuaries dedicated to Apollo of which but little is known. But the one that he puts before all the others, and which was far and away the most celebrated, was of course Delphi.

[1] Roland Crahay, *La littérature oraculaire chez Hérodote*, Paris, 1956, p. 101.

3

THE ORACLE AT DELPHI

In Phocis, in the heart of central Greece, two thousand feet above the waters of the Gulf of Corinth, with the cliffs of the Phedriades (the 'shining ones') rising sheer behind it to the Parnassus plateau, stands the site of Delphi.

The site though mountainous is in close proximity to the sea and from earliest times its majestic grandeur must have struck men's imaginations. The ancients may have talked less about natural scenery than we do, but they were probably no less sensitive to its beauties. And though no doubt the location of their temples was dictated by religious considerations, it cannot be altogether due to chance that these scarcely ever came into conflict with their unerring sense of scenic beauty, so that it is impossible to think of a single Greek sanctuary built in a dull or commonplace spot.

Going by way of the acropolis of Chryso (Krisa in ancient times) which dominates the valley and olive groves of the Pleistos, a visitor, if he is a good walker, can make the climb from the port of Itea (near the Kirrha of antiquity) on the Gulf of Corinth to the village of Delphi in little more than three hours. Alternatively he can take the overland route from Athens which crosses Boeotia and at Livadia (Lebadeia in antiquity) begins to climb the lower slopes of Parnassus, reaching Delphi from the side of the sanctuary of Athena Pronaia, situated to the east of the sanctuary of Apollo. The Pythia, though apparently secluded in her mountain retreat, was nevertheless fairly easy of access to the pilgrim.[1]

---

[1] As regards the whole question of the Delphic oracle the reader is referred to the following publications. J. Bousquet, 'Observations sur l'omphalos archaïque de Delphes', in the *Bull. Corr. hell.*, 75 (1951), pp. 210–23; H. V. Hermann, *Omphalos,* Münster, 1959, and the review of this book by J. Bousquet in *Gnomon*, 32 (1960), pp. 258–62; E. Bourguet, *Les ruines de Delphes,* Paris, 1914; F. Courby, *Fouilles de*

Between the two sanctuaries, a steep gorge cuts into the Parnassus massif at the point where the two walls of the Phedriades meet and from it flow the cool and abundant waters of the Castalia. Farther to the west there is another spring, the Cassotis, whose water was conveyed by a system of ducts to the temple of Apollo. We have already seen the importance of water in divination.

Delphi was a religious centre long before the Olympians, Apollo and Athena, appeared on the scene. Archaeological research makes it clear that dwellings and sanctuaries existed there as early as Mycenaean times. Traditions of primitive divinities, particularly the Great Goddess of the Minoans, identified with Gê (Earth), lingered on in the memory of the Greeks, as we can see from the Pythia's prayer, with which Aeschylus' *Eumenides* opens.

Before entering the temple of Apollo to pronounce her oracle, the Pythia pays homage to all the other local deities: to the first prophetess, Earth; to Themis and Phoebe who succeeded her, occupying the prophetic throne before Phoebus, that is to say, Pythian Apollo, lord of 'rocky Pytho' as Homer calls Delphi.[1] According to Aeschylus, the passing of the oracle from Earth to Apollo had taken place peacefully and by consent. Then, among the new gods who share Delphi with Apollo, the Pythia is careful not to forget Pallas Pronaia, the Nymphs of the Corycian cave (situated on the Parnassus plateau above Delphi and which tourists can visit today), Bromios (or Dionysus), Poseidon and finally Zeus, the supreme god and father of Apollo.

Euripides, who cannot resist putting Aeschylus right and reading him a lecture, gives a slightly different and probably somewhat older version. In one of the choruses from *Iphigeneia in Tauris*, he speaks of the violent struggle which

---

Delphes, ii: *La terrasse du Temple*, Paris, 1927; R. Flacelière, 'Le fonctionnement de l'oracle de Delphes au temps de Plutarque' in the *Annales de l'Ecole des Hautes Etudes de Gand*, ii (1938), pp. 69–107; P. Amandry, *La mantique apollinienne à Delphes*, Paris, 1950; R. Flacelière, 'Le délire de la Pythie est-il une légende?' in the *Rev. Et. anc.* 52 (1950), pp. 306–24; Marie Delcourt, *L'oracle de Delphes*, Paris, 1955; H. W. Parke and D. E. W. Wormell: *The Delphic Oracle*, 2 vols., Oxford, 1956, and my review of this book in the *Revue de philologie*, 32 (1958), pp. 261–67.

[1] *Iliad*, IX, 404–5.

occurred between Earth, the first mistress of the oracle, and Apollo and which was settled by Zeus in favour of his son. In this version Earth 'conjured up dreams and nocturnal visions which laid bare the past, the present and the future to countless mortals as they slept'. This oneiromancy of Earth's was an intolerable piece of rivalry to the Apollonian cult, just as night is the rival of day, for it must be remembered that Phoebus Apollo (the 'refulgent') was also the sun-god. Zeus' judgment 'liberated man from the mysteries of darkness' and bestowed on Apollo his way and his prestige.

Divination by dreams was not the only form practised at Delphi before the final triumph of Apollo and of inspired prophecy, for traces of other methods (probably very ancient in origin), particularly divination by lot, continued to survive even into classical times.

The *Homeric Hymn to Pythian Apollo* tends to corroborate Euripides' version rather than Aeschylus', for it records that the god, born at Delos, could only have established himself at Delphi after he had 'slain with his powerful bow the female Dragon, the huge and monstrous beast' which must have been the guardian of the primitive oracle of Earth. Indeed the creature associated with earth cults is invariably a dragon or a snake. In this instance, it was called the Python, which is clearly cognate with *Pytho*, with the adjective *Pythian* which was applied to Apollo as well as to the great games held at Delphi and with *Pythia*, the name by which the priestess was known.

The same poem also tells how Apollo having been turned into a dolphin (*delphis*) chose some Cretan merchants to be the first priests of his temple at Delphi. Can this be accepted as reliable evidence that divination at Delphi was influenced by the ancient Minoan civilization? According to other traditions Apollo came from the north, from Pieria, with the Hellenic or Dorian tribes who drove Homer's Achaeans out of Greece; while still others attribute his origin—was he not called the Lycian god?—to Lycia in far-away Asia. The beginnings of everything, especially of gods, are always obscure.

Amongst the other recent divinities that are referred to alongside Apollo in *The Eumenides*, Dionysus and the Nymphs merit special attention when one is seeking to explain how divination by possession originated at Delphi. According to the philosopher, Heracleitus, the Sibyl—who at Delphi was called Herophila—was wont to 'speak with a frenzied tongue' when she was prophesying, and the Pythia is also described as being beside herself when she uttered her oracles. Now, of all the gods, both the Nymphs and Dionysus were noted for their power to drive men mad; Homer speaks of the latter as 'the raving god'. High above Delphi the Maenads wandered at will on the Parnassus plateaux where the Corycian cave is dedicated to Bromios (Dionysus) and the Nymphs. When the Pythia, seated on her tripod, felt her mind darkened by the onset of prophetic frenzy she must surely have appeared much more like a Maenad than a priestess of the serene, unruffled Apollo. One has only to recall Cassandra, to whom Apollo had granted the gift of prophecy, as Aeschylus presents her in his *Agamemnon*, driven to the point of madness by the impact of the prophetic fit.

For a long time it was thought that Dionysus (only once mentioned by Homer and then in a passage in the *Iliad* that is often considered to be an interpolation) was a god who had reached Greece much later than Apollo. Modern scholars, however, believe they have discovered his name inscribed in Linear-B script on Mycenaen tablets that are considerably earlier than Homer. Thus there is no longer any justification for disregarding such evidence as supports the testimony of Aeschylus when he describes the Pythia invoking the name of Dionysus. At Delphi this god had his priestesses, the Thyiades (they may be seen today in the admirable group of three dancers carved on the capital of an acanthus column) as well as his priests, the Hosioi or Holy Ones. During the winter Apollo issued no oracles and was assumed to have left Delphi, leaving Dionysus to reign in his stead: instead of hymns to Apollo, Dionysian dithyrambs were sung. At the same time, the two cults seem to have existed happily side by side and even, in the course of time, to have become somewhat confused, since in some periods the Hosioi were regarded as priests of Apollo. There are vase paintings of the scene at Delphi in which Pythian Apollo and Dionysus are shown with their attendants on perfectly good terms with one another. Lastly, and most important, the tomb of Dionysus, the god who died and was reborn, was situated close to the tripod of Apollo in the very building where the Pythia uttered her prophecies.

Plutarch who, as the priest of Apollo at Delphi, certainly knew what he was talking about, maintains that 'as regards the Delphic oracle the part played by Dionysus was no less than Apollo's'.

* * *

Nevertheless, both in archaic and classical times, Apollo was, if not the sole, at least the principal patron of Delphi and its oracle. The date of his establishment there can be fixed approximately as not later than the eighth century B.C., since Homer already refers to him as 'lord of Pytho'. The earliest appearance of the Pythias must therefore be attributed to the seventh century at latest.

In the sanctuary of Apollo, as it was rebuilt in the sixth century after the temple had been burnt down in 548 B.C., the ancient sanctuary of Earth (Gê), near which stands the rock of the Sibyl, was divided into two by the solid wall that was then built to underpin the terrace on which the new building was to be erected. This was known as the 'temple of the Alcmaeonidae' because of the major part played in its reconstruction by the great Athenian family whom Peisistratus had banished from their country. The very lay-out of the site bears witness to the new god's victory over 'the first prophetess'.

Probably there had been inspired divination at Delphi before Apollo's coming, but it was the Apolline priesthood which henceforward took charge of its manifestations. Far from attempting to suppress prophetic ecstasy, they sanctified and institutionalized it: the Sibyl of antiquity became the Pythia, that is to say a priestess controlled by the priests and *prophetes* (a kind of temple official), while consultations were only permitted at longer and longer intervals, the dates being fixed in advance to correspond with the religious festivals of Apollo.

The origin of divination at Delphi is described by Diodorus Siculus as follows: 'In ancient times it was the goats who first discovered the oracle, which is why in our day the people of Delphi still prefer a goat when they offer sacrifice before a consultation. The discovery is said to have come about in the following manner. At the spot where the *adyton* of the present temple is there was once a chasm in the ground, where before Delphi was yet a city the goats used to graze. Whenever one of them approached this chasm and looked down into it, she would begin leaping about in an amazing fashion and bleating in a quite different voice to her normal one. And when the shepherd, marvelling at this prodigious behaviour, examined the chasm to find out what caused it, he himself was affected in the same way as the goats, who in truth behaved for all the world like people possessed, and began to prophesy the future. Later, news of what happened to those who visited the chasm began to spread among the peasants, and they flocked to the spot in large numbers, anxious to put the miracle to the test; and whenever one of them drew near he fell into a trance. Thus it was that the place itself came to be regarded as miraculous, and they believed that the oracle came to them from Gê, the Earth goddess. For a time, those who came thither to seek advice used to proclaim oracles to one another. But, later on, when many people in their ecstasy had hurled themselves into the chasm and disappeared, it seemed good to those who lived in those parts that, for the protection of others, one woman should be appointed as the sole prophetess, who alone should pronounce the oracles. They therefore constructed a device so that she could sit in safety when the spirit entered her and utter her oracles to those who sought advice from her. This device was supported by three legs, hence its name, tripod; and indeed the bronze tripods that we have today resemble it almost exactly.'

As I have already pointed out, it would be a great mistake to assume that Pythian Apollo was permanently at the disposition of his clients, despite what Lucian may say. In the earliest

9. Kleroterion: an allotment machine. Third century B.C.

10. Early Apulian volute krater. Orestes taking refuge at the omphalos in Delphi, *c.* 370 B.C. *Museo Nazionale, Naples*

11. The Theatre and the Temple of Apollo at Delphi

12. The Temple of Apollo at Delphi

period the Pythia only pronounced formal oracles from the *adyton* once a year, on the anniversary of Apollo's birth, the seventh day of the month of Bysios, that is to say at the beginning of spring, in March or April. Later, she did so on every seventh day of the month (Apollo was the 'seventh' god), except during the three winter months. But special consultations could always be arranged, I imagine, at any time except on days in the religious calendar which were regarded as inauspicious. It has also been suggested, not improbably, that in the same way that religious feast-days were gradually extended, so too the days before and after the seventh of the month would have come to be regarded as suitable for consultation. Moreover, it is probable that the Pythia was prepared to pronounce oracles by lot at any time, provided the day was auspicious.

Anybody who wanted to consult the oracle, whether in a private capacity or as delegate from a city, had first to pay a fee, known as the *pelanos*. In Euripides' *Ion*, the young servant of the temple says to the Athenian women who have come to Delphi with their queen, Creusa: 'If you have offered the sacred cake (*pelanos*) in the temple and wish to consult Apollo, draw near these altars. But do not enter the inner sanctuary until the sacrificial animals have been slain.'

Thus the *pelanos* was a preliminary offering that entitled clients to approach the altar where the blood sacrifice, to be described in a moment, would be offered up later. In Euripides, the word *pelanos* seems to have preserved its original meaning of a 'cake'. But at Delphi as at other shrines, after a cash payment had been substituted for the cake, the same name continued to be used. From one of the inscriptions at Delphi we know the terms that were agreed between the city of Apollo and the people of Phaselis in distant Lycia: 'The Phaselites will pay the *pelanos* to the Delphians according to the following tariff: for matters of state, 7 drachmas 2 obols; for private enquiries, 4 obols.' Since there were six obols to the drachma, this means that the consultation fee for a city was eleven times what private individuals had to pay.

A consultation, whether customary or specially arranged,

could not take place unless a preliminary test had shown that
the god was present and was prepared to be questioned. In
order to discover this it seems that, in the earliest period, it
sufficed to study the flight of birds, as may be seen from the
Homeric Hymn to Hermes (II, 543–9). But as the sacrifice of
animals assumed increasing importance and ornithomancy
gave way to observation of the entrails (see Chapter 1), such
sacrifices came to be preferred. In Euripides' *Ion* as Creusa's
husband, Xuthos, is about to enter the temple to consult the
oracle, he says: 'I cross the threshold, knowing indeed that on
behalf of the clients a common sacrifice has just been offered
upon the altar. And now, the day being propitious, I desire to
question the god.'

But it is Plutarch, the priest of Apollo, who provides the
most detailed account of this testing of the god's presence by
sacrificing a goat. (That it *was* usually a goat is clear from the
passage from Diodorus Siculus quoted above; and even today
flocks of goats are still plentiful in the neighbourhood of
Delphi and mount Olympus). He tells us: 'When the priests
and Hosioi make ready the victim for sacrifice, sprinkling her
with water and observing the trembling of her limbs, what
sign is it they seek unless it be the will of the god, whether or
no he will pronounce an oracle? Indeed, the animal to be
sacrificed must be pure and free from all taint. . . . The goat is
tested by the cold water; for they maintain that if, when she is
sprinkled with it, she remains insensible and motionless it is
because she is not in her normal state', which meant that the
god was unwilling to be consulted. 'Why is no oracle pronounced unless the whole body of the victim trembles and
shudders when she is aspersed? That she should twist her head
about as at other sacrifices will not suffice: she must tremble
all over and her limbs must twitch, otherwise they will say the
oracle is not functioning and they will not bring the Pythia to
the temple.' Needless to say, whether she trembled or not, the
goat was eventually despatched.

If the sacrifice proved to be favourable, the clients were then
admitted to the temple where they were ushered into a kind of
office, the *chresmographeion*, referred to above (p. 30). Judging

from the 'builders' accounts' known to us from inscriptions, this was little more than a simple shelter (*stega*) to protect them from sun and rain, which was built against the retaining wall on the north side of the temple. The first to be admitted were those to whom the Delphians accorded the privilege of the *promanteia*, a kind of 'priority ticket'. If there were several people with this privilege they drew lots as to who should be allowed to interrogate the oracle first, and afterwards those without it underwent the same procedure. In the opening scene of *The Eumenides*, the Pythia, having first called upon the gods, says as she prepares to enter the sanctuary: 'If there be Greeks amongst you, let them approach in the order ordained by lot, as is our rule, and I will prophesy as the god dictates.' Women were not allowed to consult the oracle themselves, but could do so through an intermediary.

The sacrifice was made by one of the two priests of Pythian Apollo, sometimes with the help of one or more of the five Hosioi. If the priests and the *prophetes* attached to them decided from the behaviour of the victim that the god was propitious, they would then go in search of the Pythia in order to 'induct' her into the temple.

* * *

Who, then, was the Pythia? Diodorus Siculus, continuing the passage already quoted, says: 'It is said that in ancient times oracles were pronounced by virgins, by virtue of their physical purity and association with Artemis; on which account they were readier to keep secret the oracles they revealed. But it is recounted that in more recent times a man from Thessally called Echecrates, coming to consult the oracle, beheld the virgin who was to utter the prophecies and falling in love with her because of her beauty, carried her off and raped her. As a result of this scandal, the Delphians decreed that for the future the prophetess should no longer be a virgin but a woman of fifty years and upward. Nevertheless, to this day she still wears the dress of a maiden in memory of the ancient prophetesses.' In so far as this anecdote is to be relied upon, it should be noted that, as we shall presently explain, the young man could not have seen the Pythia while she was actually prophesying, but only before or after as she was either entering or leaving the temple conducted by the priests.

As a matter of fact, the Pythia in *The Eumenides* is represented as a woman approaching her forties; and in the Museum at Naples there is a fine amphora inspired by Aeschylus' tragedy on which the Pythia is depicted with white hair. It is possible, however, that by the first century A.D. the ancient method of choosing the Pythias had been revived for Plutarch says: 'The woman who at present occupies the position belongs to one of the soundest and most respected families to be found in Delphi and has always led an irreproachable life, although, having been brought up in the home of poor peasants, when she fulfils her prophetic role she does so quite artlessly and without any special knowledge or talent. Like the young wife Xenophon describes in his *Oeconomica*, who should know nothing of the world when she enters her husband's house, the Pythia is almost completely ignorant and inexperienced, so that when she approaches the gods she does so with a truly virgin heart.'

According to Euripides the Pythia was selected 'from all the women of Delphi', doubtless on account of the purity of her life; and at all times, whatever her age, from the moment that the priests appointed her she became in a sense 'the god's bride', obliged to lead a completely chaste existence and even to live as a recluse in the house provided for her, which appears to have been within the temple precinct. Says Plutarch: 'The woman is committed to a strenuous existence and for the remainder of her life must remain pure and chaste.'

In the period when the oracle enjoyed its greatest prosperity and clients were plentiful, there were as many as three Pythias at the same time: two regular ones and an understudy who had to be prepared to take the place of either of her colleagues should she become exhausted. But in Plutarch's time, when the oracle was not so thriving, one Pythia sufficed to fulfil the calls upon her office.

It seems probable that before every consultation the Pythia visited the Castalian spring in order to perform a ritual ablution so that when she approached the god she would be immaculate. Then she was brought to the temple accompanied by her train of priests, *prophetes* and clients, and passing through the vestibule (*pronaos*) entered the central building (*cella*), which contained the altar of Poseidon, the iron throne of Pindar, an *omphalos*, one or two votive tripods and the hearth on which Neoptolemus had been sacrificed. Probably it was on this hearth that the Pythia burnt the laurel leaves and barley meal. Then, still surrounded by her attendants, she entered the 'holy of holies', the subterranean chamber, where she would pronounce the true oracles of Apollo.

*   *   *

At this point, however, we are confronted by mystery, for though the excavation of the temple of Pythian Apollo was taken as far as the virgin rock, it proved to be of little help in reconstructing the building. To the French archaeologists who were responsible for the work this was a severe disappointment, for as one of them, Émile Bourguet, has said: 'Before we started digging it was reasonable to hope that we might discover amongst the ruins the disposition of the inner buildings, that we might for instance find the stairs leading down to the clients' room. We were greatly disappointed, and what took place in the very heart of the sanctuary still remains for us a mystery. Several times as we pressed ahead with the work with the utmost care and a growing sense of disquietude one idea began to force itself upon us more and more insistently: that all we should find would be the result of systematic destruction. . . . Whether it was the last of the pagans or the earliest of the Christians who had been moved, for very different motives, to destroy all traces of what may be called the material basis or mechanism of the oracle, the result was the same: the last of the Pythias had taken her secret with her.'

It is possible, however, to unravel the mystery a little with the aid of literary sources and works of art, especially vase-paintings and one or two carvings. Indeed, the prophetic precinct was depicted by many writers and artists. At Delphi the rites were not esoteric like those at Eleusis. Whereas it was forbidden on pain of death to reveal the least detail of initiation into the mysteries of Demeter or Kore, anyone who had consulted the Pythia was free to describe whatever he had seen or heard. If only Pausanias had been in less of a hurry when he visited Delphi, and had waited until a consultation occurred, there would have been nothing to prevent him from questioning the oracle and recording the whole experience. Unfortunately those texts that refer to the prophetic precinct are for the most part very obscure, and many of the vase-paintings include a large measure of fantasy and subjective interpretation.

However, now that the excavations at Claros have brought to light an extremely well preserved subterranean sanctuary, it is perhaps permissible to apply what we have learnt from them to a description of the *manteion* at Delphi, for the fact that an *omphalos* was also found in the prophetic precinct at Claros confirms that it was strongly influenced by Delphi. Even if the *manteion* at Delphi was not so extensive as that at Claros (the space available is inadequate), it seems likely that the general layout of the two precincts was more or less the same. The contents, if not the actual structure, of the Delphic *manteion* are well known: they included a golden statue of Apollo, the tomb of Dionysus, a tripod and an *omphalos*. That a statue of the god in whose name the oracles were uttered should be there was only to be expected, and Pausanias mentions it though he did not see it himself; and, as we already know, the grave of Dionysus was close to the statue. As to the tripod this was an essential accessory of Apolline divination. In the passage already quoted, Diodorus Siculus claims to explain how it first came into use, in order that the prophetess might be seated in safety, above the chasm. It was, in fact, simply a three-legged metal cooking-vessel, sometimes supported by a fourth leg attached to the curved underside of the bowl. Heracles was said to have tried to steal Apollo's prophetic tripod, and the scene was a favourite subject for sculptors and vase-painters. Thanks to a flat lid which could be fitted to the bowl the tripod could also be used as a seat, and there are many representations of the Pythia, and of Apollo himself, seated on the tripod with their feet dangling in the air.

One of the most famous of these is the splendid Vulci goblet, on which Themis is portrayed in the role of the Pythia. She is holding a laurel branch in her right hand and a cup in her left and is delivering an oracle to Aegeus, the father of Theseus, in a miniature temple, indicated by a single column supporting an entablature with a Doric frieze.

As to the *omphalos*, that is to say the umbilicus or navel of the earth, this was originally some kind of meteor which, having fallen from heaven, was itself an object of worship. It was supposed to mark the centre of the earth, the point where two eagles, simultaneously released by Zeus from either side of the earth's circumference, had met. But the *omphalos* was also a monument to the serpent Python, the ancient guardian of Earth's oracle, whom Apollo had killed; and indeed its roughly conical shape is similar to that of funerary monuments found on certain archaic graves. The *omphalos* is represented in many works of art, often but not always together with a tripod. The vase-painting on the Naples amphora depicting the opening scene of *The Eumenides* shows Orestes clasping a large *omphalos* surrounded with a network of woollen fillets, and this resembles the marble *omphalos*, probably dating from the Roman period, that was discovered at Delphi. The other and smaller *omphalos* that was also unearthed at Delphi was almost certainly carved or reshaped in medieval times and therefore does not concern us. But the fourth century builders' accounts frequently refer to work having been carried out in the temple 'near the *omphalos*'.

Another passage in Plutarch indicates that the prophetic sanctum at Delphi, like that at Claros, consisted of two separate but communicating chambers: the room for the petitioners and the *adyton* itself, which no one was allowed to enter except the Pythia. 'The room in which those who came to consult the god were seated is, not often but occasionally and at irregular intervals, filled with a sweet-smelling vapour, as though the *adyton* were emitting as from a fountain the sweetest and most precious perfumes.' Similarly, the vase-painting to which I have referred where Aegeus is shown standing opposite the Pythia though separated from her by the column, is an over-simplification, for the consultant did not actually enter the sanctum where the prophetic tripod stood.

Other passages in Plutarch make it clear that the room reserved for the consultants was underground, and almost certainly at the same level as the *adyton*. For example, he describes the amazing circumstances in which a Pythia of his own time met her death: 'Quite recently,' he says, and this almost certainly means that it occurred during his term of office as priest of Apollo, 'some foreigners having come to consult the oracle, it seems that when the sacrificial goat was sprinkled with water she remained motionless and appeared to be quite unaffected. The priests therefore redoubled their efforts, with the result that the goat was completely drenched with water and finally died in great distress. What was the effect of this upon the Pythia? According to report, having descended into the *manteion* in a state of dejection and with the greatest reluctance, as soon as she uttered her first answer it was clear from the harshness of her voice that she was wandering like a disabled ship, as though she were filled with a dumb and evil spirit. At last, in utter confusion, she sprang towards the door and with a wild and terrifying shriek threw herself to the ground, putting to flight not only the clients but also the prophet Nicandros and the Hosioi who were attending him. Returning a few moments later, they picked her up. But though she had come to her senses again, she only survived for a few days.'

Here it may be noted that when she took her place on the tripod and began to prophesy, the Pythia was not visible to the priests and clients, for they were only able to judge of what was happening from the sound of her voice. It is significant also that when the Pythia got down from the tripod and rushed towards the room where the priests and clients were sitting, Plutarch does not say that she 'ascended', but simply that she reached the door. Already in 1938 long before the *manteion* at Claros had been excavated, I had reached the following conclusion from this and other passages: 'That part of the prophetic precinct where the clients sat was at a lower level than the main body of the temple, in an underground room; and while she was prophesying the Pythia was seated at approximately the same level as the clients, though she could not be seen by them. Thus the whole precinct, though at the same level, must have been divided into two by a wall, with a door or perhaps merely a curtain through which only the Pythia was allowed to pass.' Now we have already seen (p. 29) that at Claros the two vaulted underground rooms of the *manteion* were connected by a passage, with some kind of doorway which had 'either a door or curtain'. It therefore seems to me that the Claros ruins, so admirably preserved, bear out conclusively the account of the arrangement of the Delphic sanctuary that can be gleaned from Plutarch's writings.

At Claros the *omphalos* was found in the first room, the one reserved for the clients, and it must be assumed that this was so at Delphi, though this would not exclude the possibility that there was another *omphalos* beside the tripod. As to Apollo's statue and the tomb of Dionysus, one would expect to find these in the clients' room, since the inner sanctuary at Delphi was so small that there would scarcely have been room for them. At Claros the prophet drank from the sacred well: the Pythia, as we know, drank from the fountain of Cassotis, and since this is to the north of the temple its waters must have been piped to the *adyton*.[1]

*   *   *

While it may be true to say that 'when the last of the Pythias died her secret perished with her', this is not so much because the prophetic precinct has not survived amongst the ruins of the temple of Delphi, for it is still possible to form a tolerably clear idea of its general plan and situation. It is when we try to understand the nature of the Pythia's prophetic ecstasy, how she actually came to utter the oracles, that our legitimate curiosity seems to be moving in a world of shadows.

In certain respects the Pythia of Delphi resembles Cassan-

---

[1] For the fountain of Cassotis and the way in which its waters were brought to the temple, see Jean Pouilloux, *Fouilles de Delphes*, ii, *La région nord du sanctuaire*, Paris, 1960, pp. 17–24, and the plan on p. 22.

dra; for example, the latter was loved by Apollo and the former was regarded as his bride. But there is also one essential difference between them: the Pythia was only capable of prophecy when she was seated upon her tripod in one particular spot; unlike Cassandra's, her gift was not a personal one that accompanied her wherever she might happen to be, whether in Troy or in Mycenae. Why her powers of divination were so strictly localized may be easily understood from the passages I have quoted from Diodorus and Plutarch: her inspiration was derived from the chasm, which according to every tradition was situated within the *adyton* beneath the mantic tripod. The chasm emitted a vapour (*pneuma*) which, penetrating every orifice of her body, produced in her a state of ecstasy that enabled her to ejaculate the words and cries breathed into her by the god, as though in some way Apollo took possession of her and obscured her powers of reasoning.

Now, although excavation has failed to discover the *adyton* at Delphi it has at least proved that at the spot where it must have stood there is today no fissure from which vapour could escape. Must we therefore conclude that there could never have been such a phenomenon? It is conceivable that earthquakes and landslides, which occurred at Delphi as frequently in antiquity as in our own times, may have so modified the sub-soil that the hypothetical fissure has been blocked. Nevertheless we have no conclusive objective evidence that at any previous period there had been some kind of chemical exhalation from beneath the *adyton*.

Attempts have therefore been made to find some other explanation of the Pythia's prophetic powers. We have already noted that various types of inductive, as well as intuitive, divination were practised at Delphi, both before and after the coming of Apollo. One of these was divination by lot, or cleromancy. Now, in 1939, Amandry published a very important inscription from Delphi: a treaty between the city of Pythian Apollo and Skiathos that fixed (as in the case of Phaselis already referred to) the value of the *pelanos*, the fee that had to be paid before the oracle could be consulted. It says: 'If anyone presents himself for a consultation by two beans, the fee for a state question shall be one Aeginitan stater.' This proves that in the first half of the fourth century B.C., the date of the inscription, it was possible to arrange for a consultation 'by two beans', that is to say, by lot, and it may reasonably be assumed that it was the Pythia herself who was responsible for actually drawing the lot.

To argue from this that the whole business of consulting the Pythia in the *adyton* was nothing but make-believe, and that all she did was, in effect, to call heads or tails, would be a bold step to take, though it is tempting to do so because, as we have seen, the theory of inspiration by some kind of vapour is open to considerable doubt. When he published this inscription, however, Amandry was careful not to go as far as this: quite rightly he drew a clear distinction between 'consultations by beans' and 'consultations in the *adyton*' and though both kinds may have occurred in the same place we cannot be certain of this. He prudently said: 'It cannot be assumed that the lot-oracle was the only method practised. Indeed, the text itself implies that it was not: for if there had been but one mode of revelation it would have been enough simply to state the fee "for admission to the *manteion*". The words "if one presents oneself . . ." suggest a parallel formula which, with the following phrase (had the text not been mutilated), would have introduced a clause relating to the other "method of consultation", that is, inspired by possession.'

Once again we may turn to Plutarch. 'The Thessalians,' he writes, 'having sent the beans to the god at Delphi that he might choose a king, Aleuas' uncle, without the knowledge of his father, included the name of Aleuas in the draw. When the Pythia drew forth his name, his father denied having put in the bean with his son's name on it and everyone concluded that some mistake had been made in inscribing the beans.' This makes it clear that when people wished to consult the Pythia by lot—a kind of consultation 'on the cheap'—they themselves prepared in advance the beans from which the prophetess had to choose. Thus there could be no question of any sort of clandestine drawing of lots taking the place of what they believed to be an inspired prophecy; or of the latter being preceded by some kind of duplication of the arrangements. Nor is the hypothesis of trickery on the part of the priests enough to explain everything; particularly when we remember that all a lot-oracle could do was, as in this case, to choose one of several names, or pick out one of several proposed solutions to a problem. It would have been quite incapable of providing an answer to the much more complex questions which, as we know, many consultants used to put to the Pythia.

All our sources confirm that when the Pythia was prophesying she was in a state of frenzy. Plutarch, as we have seen, attributed the death of the Pythia during his lifetime to noxious fumes (*pneuma*), and before this Plato had said in his *Phaedrus*: 'It is to their madness that we owe the many benefits that the Pythia of Delphi and the priestesses of Dodona were able to bestow upon Greece both privately and in public life, for when they were in their right minds their achievements amounted to little or nothing.' The word that Cicero uses in *De Divinatione* to describe this prophetic madness was *furor*. It was very far from being a state of grace, or of serenity: divine possession manifested itself in a condition of frenzied agitation. True, Lucan's description in *De Bello Civile* (v, 169–218) is obviously overdone, but it is no more than poetic exaggeration of a reality that was in itself sufficiently amazing.

If we reject the highly debatable *pneuma*, is there any other material agent that could have helped produce this extraordinary condition? We know that the Pythia chewed laurel leaves (the tree of Apollo) and that certain species of laurel are poisonous. But this line of thought is scarcely worth pursuing: to the prophet of Claros no exhalation from the soil was available, and whether or not he chewed laurel leaves we do not know. All he did was to drink from the well in the *adyton*, as the Pythia drank from the fountain of Cassotis, and it was this water, which according to the excavators of Claros was perfectly safe to drink, that was said to be the cause of his inspiration.

In our own times, as in antiquity, states of religious exaltation or frenzy can be induced without recourse to any physical agent. (I am thinking, for example, of the 'Anastenaria'.) We may therefore reject the *pneuma* theory and yet accept the Pythia's madness as genuine, as a religious phenomenon, not necessarily hysteria but similar to what we call self-hypnotism or auto-suggestion. However, if we wish to understand this aspect of divination it is perhaps more helpful to read a novel like Pär Lagerkvist's *The Sibyl* than most erudite historical studies of the subject.[1]

*   *   *

We saw above (p. 30) that at Branchidae, after the prophetess had been questioned the clients left the temple and returned to the *chresmographeion*. There an official record of the consultation was drawn up and, when the god's answer had been redrafted in solemn terms, usually in verse, the consultants received a copy of it. In all probability pretty well the same procedure was followed at Delphi, though precisely where it took place is not known. It may well have been that the rough shelter built against the wall of the terrace in which the consultants foregathered may also have served as the oracle's 'office'. In any case, those members of the priesthood described in the sources as *prophetes* were with the clients in the *manteion* and were responsible for editing the oracles.

It has even been suggested that these Delphic *prophetes* were in fact the real authors of the oracles; that they drafted them *before* the consultation, immediately they discovered what questions were to be asked, and then informed the Pythia what answers she should give. In my opinion this hypothesis is unacceptable. In particular, it conflicts with the literary evidence that on several occasions attempts were made to corrupt the Pythia; as was the case with Alacmaeonidae, for example, and with Cleomenes king of Sparta. The fact that occasionally, in the hope of receiving a favourable answer, people sought to bribe the Pythia, and not the priests, can only mean that it was

---

[1] For the *Anasténaria*, see the remarkable study by C. A. Romaios published by the French Institute in Athens in their *Cahiers d'hellénisme*, I, 1949: 'Cultes populaires de la Thrace, les Anasténaria, la cérémonie du Lundi pur'; see also Jeanne and Georges Roux, *Grèce*, pp. 167–68 and the photographs, Paris, 1957.

she who was primarily responsible for the oracle; and in such cases, moreover, it was she who was dismissed.

Yet she was a simple peasant woman, with little learning or culture: it was because of her moral character that she was chosen, not because of any education she may have had. It is impossible therefore to attribute to her the verse-form in which the oracles were couched (usually in epic hexameters), heavy and ill-contrived though most of them were. Indeed, the Epicureans considered these verses to be so unworthy of Apollo, the patron of the Muses, that they used this as an argument to support their scepticism about oracles. Moreover, when uttering her prophecies the Pythia is said to have expressed herself in wild, onomatopoeic cries as well as articulate speech, and this 'raw material' certainly had to be interpreted and worked over. The fact of the matter is that the oracle was produced as the result of collaboration between the Pythia, the inspired medium, and the temple officials who were responsible for giving it its final form.

One copy of the oracle was then handed to the consultant (who, if he was representing a city, had to report faithfully to his principals) and another was kept in the Delphic archives, the *zygastron* referred to in inscriptions. Whether only authentic answers were kept in the *zygastron* or whether fictitious oracles produced after the event for propaganda purposes were also preserved is a matter that raises the whole question of the professional honesty of the priesthood; a question that cannot be answered.

It is rather surprising that so few oracles should have been discovered amongst the inscriptions at Delphi. Their rarity suggests that normally the oracles were not 'posted' in the sanctuary. The answers given to Lycurgus the Spartan legislator, and to Croesus the famous king of Lydia, seem to have been seen at Delphi in the fifteenth century by Cyriac of Ancona, but as they have not since been found one cannot help wondering whether Cyriac may not have simply copied them from Herodotus. All that we have today are the oracle given to Agamemnon and a poem about 'the miracle of the hair' which is not properly speaking an oracular answer at all.

In this respect, some of Apollo's other sanctuaries have been more productive than that of Delphi. However, literary sources—Herodotus above all, but also Plutarch—have preserved many of the Delphic oracles, and inscriptional evidence from archaeological sites has produced others; for example, those relating to the poet Archilocus from the island of Paros.

The question arises: are these oracles, as bequeathed to us by ancient writers and inscriptions, really genuine? By which I mean, do they retain exactly the same form that they were given by the priests of Delphi immediately after the consultation in the *adyton*? It would take a bold man either to answer this affirmatively or completely to deny their authenticity. The work that has so far been done on this question has in most cases arrived at no definite conclusion and probably never will. And it is easy to understand why. On the one hand, the prestige of the Delphic oracle, at least up to the time of the Persian wars, was so great that cities as well as private individuals would have been sorely tempted either to modify an authentic oracle or to produce a complete forgery; we shall see some concrete examples of this in the next chapter. On the other hand, since the Greeks were never lacking in the spirit of criticism, how could they have believed in these oracles if some of them at least had not been authentic? Theoretically, the *zygastron* at Delphi would have made it possible to test the truth of the oracles, provided of course that it did not contain answers invented by the priests for purposes of propaganda; and there is no evidence that the Delphic priesthood ever committed forgery. But even in the case of an authentic oracle it is not to be supposed that the answer was always clear and precise. It was not for nothing that Apollo was nicknamed Loxias, the Ambiguous One. Often enough the answers were completely enigmatic, and it required all the skill of the official interpreters, the *exegetes*, to make sense of them; and the same oracle might well be interpreted in different and even contradictory ways. The Greeks always delighted in such mental gymnastics.

Commenting on the fact that in his day the oracles were in simple prose whereas for so long they had been versified,

Plutarch went as far as to say that the priests welcomed the obscurity inherent in verse because of the protection this afforded them. 'It would not surprise me', he writes, 'if in ancient times some measure of ambiguity, of indirectness and obscurity, was sometimes considered to be necessary. For it was not just a question of some individual person consulting the oracle about the purchase of a slave or some other private matter, but of very powerful cities, kings and tyrants with mighty ambitions, seeking the god's advice on important issues. To anger or annoy such men by harsh truths that conflicted with their desires would have had its disadvantages for the priests of the oracle. . . . Thus the god protected them and took care that in fulfilling their duties they did not risk becoming the victims of wicked men. For this reason Apollo, though not prepared to conceal the truth, manifests it in roundabout ways: by clothing it in poetic form he rids it of what is harsh or offensive, as one does with a brilliant light by reflecting it and thus splitting it into several rays. As for the answers given to ordinary people, it was also sometimes advisable that these should be concealed from their oppressors or hidden from their enemies. Thus these too were wrapped up in circumlocution and equivocation so that the meaning of the oracle, while hidden from others, could always be grasped by those whom it concerned if they applied themselves to unravelling it.' On the other hand, in his day, Plutarch continues: 'The oracle is no longer concerned with complicated or secret matters. The questions she is asked have to do with people's everyday concerns: shall they get married, or make such and such a journey, or lend some money; while the most important consultations on the part of cities are concerned with the harvest, or stock raising, or public health.' Under these circumstances all circumlocution and obscurity became unnecessary.

*　　　*　　　*

'None of the consultations for which we have inscriptional evidence', says Amandry, 'was earlier than the Peloponnesian war. Herodotus himself, though the earliest of our sources,

13. The omphalos at Delphi

14. Athenian volute krater. Apollo enthroned at Delphi, 440–430 B.C.
Found at Spina, Italy

15. Krater depicting the meeting of Apollo and Dionysus

16. Roman omphalos *Delphi Museum*

was already too late, for, by the middle of the fifth century
B.C., the period when oracles enjoyed their greatest prestige
was already over. Divination seems to have reached its peak
in the sixth century. It was then that the temple of Delphi,
which had been begun two centuries earlier, was finally
completed.'[1]

Indeed, in the sixth century almost every Greek city of any
importance—in southern Italy, in Asia Minor and the Black
Sea, as well as in Greece itself—had its temple to Pythian
Apollo, crammed with precious gifts. Even barbarians like
Croesus king of Lydia sent their representatives to question
the oracle and loaded Delphi with costly presents in token of
their gratitude. According to the wealth of their donors, these
offerings might take the form of sumptuous monuments or
modest votive gifts, but all of them bore witness to the
gratitude of the consultants for the advice of the Pythia and
to their devotion to Apollo.

Thus the fame of the Pythian oracle extended far beyond the
limits of the Greek world, for men like Croesus and Midas
sent their envoys from Lydia and Phrygia. One of the predictions the Pythia made to the former reads: 'When a mule shall
be king of the Medes, then, O Lydian, flee and have no shame
for your cowardice.' Croesus may well be excused for not
having understood in time that the mule was Apollo's way of
referring to Cyrus, the founder of the Persian empire. The
result was disastrous for him for, according to Herodotus,
encouraged by this oracle he decided to resist his powerful
neighbour. Only after he had been defeated and taken prisoner
did he understand too late the allusion to Cyrus who, like the
mule, was of mixed race, his mother being a native of Medea of
noble birth while his father belonged to a modest Persian family.

When the temple of Apollo was destroyed by fire in 548,
the Amphictyons, who were then administering the sanctuary,
appealed to the entire Greek world for money to rebuild it.
There was a wide response, and even the king of Egypt,
Amasis, sent a valuable contribution.

[1] P. Amandry, 'Oracles, littérature et politique' (*Rev. Et. anc.*, 61, 1959, pp.
400–13).

The Pylaeo-Delphic Amphictyony (so called because it had originated at Thermopylae before taking root at Delphi) was a regional federation of several peoples from the neighbourhood of the two temples, that of Demeter at Thermopylae and that of Apollo at Delphi. About 600 B.C., at the instigation of the Athenian, Solon, the Amphictyons declared a Holy War against the city of Kirrha, where some pilgrims had been held to ransom. The city was captured by the coalition and, with its port, razed to the ground; its land was proclaimed to be the property of the god. It was shortly after this first Holy War (of which there were several others) that the Pythian Games, held at Delphi every four years, were reorganized, and henceforward assumed an importance for the whole of Greece comparable to those at Olympia.

The oracle attracted crowds of people from all parts of the country, and no city dared to embark upon any large-scale enterprise without having first sought its advice. For example, it played an important, though not easily explained, part in the great movement of Greek colonization. It seems to have furnished the founders of new cities not only with ritual laws for the religious cults and institutions to be established overseas, but also with practical information about the geography of the far-away countries to which they were going. It is easy to see why Delphi should have become an admirable centre of information, since pilgrims flocked there from all parts of the Mediterranean, especially at the time of the Pythian Games.

According to Jéan Bérard: 'As on every other great occasion when the ancient Greeks had difficulty in making up their minds on either a public or private issue, the Delphic oracle was often consulted by the founders of new towns. In many cases tradition has preserved for us an account of these consultations, sometimes even the actual text of the answer, whether right or wrong, that the Pythia was supposed to have given to the leaders of the future cities. Almost from the start the Pythia appears to have encouraged these expeditions to new countries: she did so, for example, in the case of Cumae, of Rhegion, Syracuse, Crotona and Tarentum. As regards Rhegion it even seems that the Messenians and the Chalchideans, its joint founders, were brought together in the first place by the priests of Delphi. But it is clear that, if the Pythia was able to give useful information about the regions to be colonized and the sites to be selected, as she did for Rhegion, Syracuse, Crotona and Tarentum, it was only because she herself had previously received the information from those who had already explored the new sea routes and founded settlements there.'[1]

Here is a typical example, the oracle given to the Spartan Phalanthos, the founder of Tarentum, as recorded by Pausanias: 'Having been chosen to command the colonists, Phalanthos received an oracle from Delphi according to which, as soon as he felt rain from a clear sky, he was to seize the country and the town. He did not immediately grasp the meaning of the oracle, nor did he take the precaution of having it explained by a professional *exegetes*. At the head of his ships he landed in Italy, where he won several victories over the inhabitants but failed either to capture a town or to gain possession of a district. Then, remembering the oracle, it struck him that what the god had predicted was impossible since it could never rain so long as the sky remained clear and cloudless. Feeling disheartened, his wife, who had accompanied him on the expedition, sought to comfort him: she laid his head upon her knees and began delousing his hair. While she was thus engaged, convinced that the position her husband was in was unlikely to improve, out of tenderness for him she began to weep. And when Phalanthos felt her tears falling upon his head, immediately he understood the meaning of the prophecy: for his wife's name was Aithra, that is to say "clear sky". The following night, therefore, he attacked Tarentum, the greatest and most prosperous of all the coastal towns, and captured it from the barbarians.'

Up to the time of the Persian wars the authority of the oracle seems to have been practically undisputed. At the time of the invasion of Xerxes, the attitude of the Pythia was scarcely encouraging for the defenders of Greek liberty. The king's

---

[1] J. Bérard: *L'expansion et la colonisation grecques jusqu'aux guerres médiques*, Paris, 1960, p. 62.

envoys, who were sent to demand 'earth and water' in token of submission and to organize intelligence for the Medes throughout Greece, may perhaps have been welcomed at Delphi, for the cities belonging to the Amphictyony, almost all of which lay to the north of Thermopylae and were therefore the first to be threatened, had declared in favour of the invader. Be this as it may, the Pythia predicted nothing but misfortune for the Greeks. When the battles of Salamis and Plataea drastically changed the situation, an attempt was made to explain that her oracles—particularly the one that had proclaimed the wooden fortress to be impregnable—had in fact foreseen and facilitated these victories, and gifts from the victorious Greeks flowed into the temple of Apollo.

The political independence of the sanctuary may be said to have come to an end with the Persian wars. Henceforward the oracle was to be under the patronage of whichever state achieved the hegemony: Athens in the fifth century, then Sparta, Thebes and Macedonia in the fourth, the Aetolians in the third, and finally the Romans. Nevertheless it was to continue to exert a considerable influence, at least up to the time of Alexander the Great; as will be remembered, the latter insisted upon going to Delphi before setting out on his conquests in order to have himself proclaimed invincible by the Pythia.

The Delphic oracle's chief claim to fame was, however, the moral and intellectual influence that it exerted. Busts of Homer and Hesiod, as well as Pindar's iron seat, were kept in the temple of Pythian Apollo. During the latter's lifetime the oracle had instructed the Delphians to grant him part of the tithes dedicated to the god. Apollo, patron of the Muses, was the natural patron of poetry and poets, and this was not forgotten by the Pythia. He was also the protector of the sciences, and he was supposed to have told the inhabitants of the sacred island of Delos to double the cubic capacity of an altar in order to oblige them to study geometry: they must have had their work cut out since doubling the cube is as insoluble a problem as squaring the circle. Lastly, the philosophical maxims inspired by Apollo were carved in the porch of the temple: 'Measure in all things', 'Know thyself', 'To commit oneself is to court misfortune'. According to Plutarch, the Pythia's inspiration extended beyond the moral domain to include metaphysics: in one of her oracles she confirmed the immortality of the soul, as Socrates did in Plato's *Phaedo*.[1] Socrates used to advise his disciples that, whenever they were at a loss, they should consult the Pythia. It was he who recommended Xenophon to visit Delphi before taking part in the expedition of the Ten Thousand, though, as he was passionately anxious to go, instead of asking the oracle whether he should or not Xenophon merely asked which of the gods he should sacrifice to in order to ensure that the expedition should be to his benefit. Such attempts to trick the god were by no means uncommon.

The philosophical significance that Socrates derived from the Delphic maxim 'Know thyself' is well known. When his friend Cherephon consulted the Pythia to find out whether there was anyone in the world wiser than Socrates the oracle replied that no such man existed.[2] It is not surprising therefore that Plato, the disciple of Socrates, attributed such an important function to the Delphic oracle in the organization of his ideal city. As he says in *The Republic*: 'It is to Apollo, the god of Delphi, that it falls to decree the most important, the noblest and the first of laws: those which concern the building of temples, the offering of sacrifices and all things affecting the worship of the gods, of the spirits and of the heroes, as well as the graves of the dead and the honours that we should render them that they may be propitious to us. For these are things of which we are ignorant and, as founders of a Republic, we shall if we are wise seek advice about them only from him, accepting no one else as our guide. For this god, the traditional exponent of religion, sits at the very centre and navel of the earth to instruct the human race.' This passage is fully borne out by *The Laws* in which, right at the end of his life, Plato was once again to express his complete confidence in the Delphic oracle with regard to all religious and moral questions.

[1] For the moral influence of Delphi, see Jean Defradas, *Les Thèmes de la propagande delphique*, Paris, 1954.

[2] This particular oracle is discussed in a book by Ph.-E. Legrand: *Mélanges Perrot* (1903), pp. 213-22.

4

DIVINATION AND POLITICS

As we saw in the previous chapter, the attitude of the Pythia towards the Persian war reveals the extent to which the oracle of Delphi was in danger of becoming involved and, as a result, compromised in the backwash of war and diplomacy. In fact the oracle was consulted on all serious issues, particularly political matters affecting the cities. Even had it remained utterly impartial it would have been suspected of putting the interests of one state, or group of states, above those of another; and from what we know of the history of ancient Greece there is little to suggest that the oracle *was* impartial. Moreover, it must be remembered that the ancients had no idea of the distinction between spiritual and temporal matters that we make today: priests and prophets were as much entitled to be magistrates and government officials as were generals or tax-collectors. In the modern epoch, when this distinction is generally accepted in the western world, at least in theory, we know only too well how fluid is the boundary between the two and how easily it may be overstepped. In antiquity even this theoretical distinction did not exist.

The close connection between politics and religion mainly revealed itself with regard to divination, and, particularly in the case of the oracles, appeared both natural and inevitable. In periods of profound and widespread religious faith, as in Greece until the appearance of the sophists about the middle of the fifth century, one already comes across signs of this interpenetration. But later, as religion began to lose its hold except upon the common people, these noticeably increase, for oracles, whether true or false, were becoming for an increasing number of ambitious politicians the most effective and often the simplest means of propaganda in support of their aims.

And here it should be noted that, though it was usual for the magistrates of a city to send delegates to consult the oracles on their behalf, on occasion they themselves would visit the sanctuary. This, it would seem, was the custom in Sparta, where it was the ephors themselves who used to consult the oracle of Pasiphae at Thalamai, which was not far from Lacedaemonia. Indeed, in his *Lives of Agis and Cleomene*, Plutarch describes how 'one of the ephors, falling asleep at the shrine of Pasiphae [where the revelation took place by incubation, as at Epidaurus], had an extraordinary dream: he dreamt that in the room where the ephors met to conduct their business four of the five seats had been overturned. Shocked by this vision he heard a voice from the sanctuary announcing that this was in the interest of Sparta.' When he got back to Sparta the ephor reported what he had seen and heard to king Cleomenes III. At first the king, who had been planning to get rid of the ephors, was greatly disturbed, for he assumed that the ephor must have suspected his intentions and had invented this dream in order to sound him out. But having convinced himself of the man's sincerity he took heart and, in order not to give the oracle the lie, he carried out his original plan: he gave orders for all the ephors to be killed, and of the five only one escaped with his life. This took place in the year 227 B.C.

*   *   *

By about the sixth century we begin to encounter those disquieting characters known as *chresmologues,* collectors and peddlers of oracles who used to trade in prophecies old and new and were quite capable of unscrupulously altering existing oracles, or even of producing new ones to order, to please their clients. Herodotus tells us of a certain Athenian, Onoma-crites: 'He was a *chresmologue* who compiled oracles in the name of Musaeus, and was expelled from Athens by Hipparchus, son of Peisistratus, after being caught red-handed inserting in the Musaeus archive an oracle announcing that the neighbouring island of Lemnos would disappear into the sea. Previously, however, Hipparchus and he had been on very intimate terms.' Indeed, Peisistratus and his son were well known as amateur collectors of oracles: in 510 B.C. Cleomenes obtained possession of a collection of prophecies that had once belonged to them, notable amongst which were several oracles predicting that Athens would achieve important victories over Sparta. Whether Hipparchus was annoyed with Onomacrites' interpolation because it was a forgery or because it conflicted with the Athenian government's plans as regards the Hellespont (the Straits through which corn had to be imported) is something we shall never know.

The fact remains, however, that after his banishment from Athens Onomacrites took refuge in Susa (as Themistocles was to do later), where before long he was joined by Peisistratus and his family, who in their turn had been banished by the Athenians with the help of Sparta in 510 B.C. 'There,' Herodotus continues, 'whenever Onomacrites appeared in the presence of the Persian king the Peisistratidae would speak of him in flattering terms [the "planting" of the document had either been forgiven or forgotten] while he himself would recite oracles. If he happened to come upon one announcing a defeat for the barbarians he would pass it over in silence, preferring to quote only those that were auspicious: for instance, that a Persian was destined to throw a bridge across the Hellespont, or indicating the route to be taken by the expedition. Thus, by proclaiming these oracles, he was able to influence Xerxes.'

During the time when Peisistratus and his son were in control of Athens, the noble and wealthy family of the Alcmaeonidae was banished, and fled to Delphi. There they set about winning the good graces of the Delphic priesthood by loading them with gifts; for example they contributed liberally to the rebuilding of the temple of Apollo, which had been destroyed in 548 B.C. It is not surprising therefore that the Pythia issued a number of oracles urging the Spartans to make war upon Athens and drive out the tyrants, since this would enable the Alcmaeonidae to return to their fatherland. The Spartans appear to have been most reluctant to intervene and it was only because of pressure from the oracle that they eventually decided to declare war. After an initial setback the oracle ordered them to persevere, and the second expedition they despatched was eventually crowned with success. In 510, thanks to this assistance Pythian Apollo had obtained for them from Sparta, the Alcmaeonidae were able to return to Athens. This story clearly shows what astonishing authority the oracle exercised at this period, but it also indicates the extent to which the Delphic priesthood and the Pythia could be influenced by personal pressure, political intrigue and financial generosity, and this state of affairs quite obviously contained the seeds of decline.

The Spartan army that drove Hippias out of Athens was commanded by Cleomenes I, who later quarrelled with his co-ruler Demaratus. Now there was some doubt about the legitimacy of Demaratus, and one of the parties in Sparta maintained that he was not really the son of king Ariston. 'As this issue gave rise to violent dissension', Herodotus says, 'the Spartans decided to ask the Delphic oracle whether in fact Demaratus was Ariston's son. This idea of appealing to the Pythia had however already been considered by Cleomenes and he had therefore taken steps to win over to his side Cobon, son of Aristophantos, a man of great influence at Delphi; and Cobon persuaded the prophetess, Perialla, to say whatever Cleomenes wished her to say. Thus, when she was questioned by the delegates, the Pythia announced that Demaratus was not the son of Ariston. But in the end this plot was exposed: Cobon had to leave Delphi, and the prophetess Perialla was deprived of her honours and her position.'

In the fifth century, the best-known and most influential seer in Athens was Lampo, a friend of Pericles who, according to Glotz, appointed him to be a kind of 'secretary of state for religion'. He was thus an important official. In particular, as chief *exegetes*, he was responsible for interpreting religious law and ritual, as well as the oracles. Now the law relating to the offering of the first-fruits at Eleusis contains an amendment proposed by Lampo. It is therefore certain that he played a decisive part in what Glotz calls 'this curious essay in political propaganda disguised as religion by which Athens was attempting, in an unusually conciliatory manner, to induce the whole of Greece to accept her as the true and only source of corn and civilization.'[1] Lampo was also concerned in another of Pericles' panhellenic enterprises: the founding of the Italian colony of Thurii, the new Sybaris. Together with the architect Hippodamos of Miletus, who was in charge of building the town, the *exegetes* was responsible for advising the expedition and making sure that the city was founded under good auspices and observed all the appropriate rites. Thucydides, indeed, refers to Lampo as one of the leading Athenians who negotiated and put into effect the Peace of Nicias and later arranged the alliance with Sparta. In the following chapter we shall come across him again, involved in a controversy with the philosopher Anaxagoras, another friend of Pericles.

The incident that resulted in the dismissal of the Pythia Perialla was not the only occasion on which the Spartans had recourse to divination in order to settle a problem of the royal succession arising from disputed paternity. While Agis king of Sparta was with his army at Decelea in Attica, his wife Timaea was seduced by Alcibiades, who had been banished from Athens and was temporarily living in Lacedaemonia. Their liaison was discovered when, in the middle of an earthquake in the winter of 413–412, Alcibiades was seen leaving Timaea's room. The child she bore nine months later was named Leotychidas, though in secret Timaea used to call him Alcibiades, after his real father. Agis was fully aware of what had happened and did not regard the boy as his son but, says Plutarch, 'during the king's last illness, Leotychidas threw himself at his feet and persuaded him by his tears to recognize him as his son in the presence of several witnesses. However, after the death of Agis, Lysander, who by virtue of defeating Athens had become the most influential man among the Spartans, led a campaign to put Agis' brother Agesilaus, on the throne, insisting that it was impermissible for a bastard like Leotychidas to be king. . . . Now at that time there was in Sparta a chres-

---

[1] For Lampo, as well as for the *exegetes* and the chresmologues, see James H. Oliver, *The Athenian Expounders of the Sacred and Ancestral Law*, Baltimore, 1950. The decree referring to the first fruits to be offered at Eleusis is I.G. I^2 76 = Syll.[3] 83 = Tod: *A Selection of Greek Historical Inscriptions*, 74. My quotations from G. Glotz are taken from his *Histoire grecque*, VOL. II, pp. 169 and 176–7.

mologue called Diopeithes who was simply bursting with
ancient prophecies and was looked upon as being well versed
in divine matters. He declared that Agesilaus, being lame,
could not become king of Sparta, and in proof of this he produced before the tribunal the following oracle:

> Despite your pride, O Sparta, take good care
> Lest there be born from thee a limping reign:
> Else shalt thou suffer many a weary year
> Woes unforeseen and war's destructive blast.

Against this, Lysander argued that, if the Spartans were
frightened by this oracle, it was Leotychidas they should
beware of, for the god would scarcely concern himself about
a lame king, whereas to raise a bastard to the throne instead
of a member of the Heraclidae would be to lame the kingdom
itself, since one of the two kings would then be legitimate and
the other a bastard.'

In the end, thanks to Lysander, it was Agesilaus who
became king. But Plutarch, who quotes the oracle referred to
by Diopeithes in his *Lives* of Agesilaus and of Lysander, as
well as in the dialogue *On the Pythian Oracles*, seems to have
believed in it completely. And, indeed the reign of Agesilaus
(401–360) was in fact remarkable for the number of wars,
culminating in the victories of Epaminondas during the last
decade of his reign, that turned out unfavourably for the
Spartans, who in 371 lost to the Thebans the hegemony that
Lysander had achieved thirty years earlier.

*   *   *

According to Nilsson, 'the influence of the seers was less
important than that of the many peddlers of oracles, the
chresmologues, who circulated amongst the people oracles that
were either anonymous or else attributed to ancient prophets
like Musaeus and Bakis or to some famous sanctuary. Such
oracles were not messages from the gods, uttered in response
to sacrifice or in some similar manner, but simply doggerel
verses which the Greeks learnt by heart and passed on by word
of mouth. It goes without saying that, when some important
issue had to be decided, they provided a powerful means of

influencing public opinion. In this respect the role of the oracles and seers has as a rule been underestimated, for as regards political agitation it was comparable to that of newspapers and political pamphlets today.'[1]

By the time of the Peloponnesian war (431–404 B.C.) the sophists had to some extent begun to undermine religious belief, at least at certain levels of society, though the mass of the people retained their faith. This was, however, if we are to believe the historian Thucydides and the comic poet Aristophanes, the golden age of the chresmologues.

Clearly, Thucydides himself had little faith in oracles, though he refers to them again and again on account of their far from negligible influence. When the Spartans, almost always the most devoted clients of Pythian Apollo and the most obedient to his oracles, consulted the Pythia about the outcome of the war, she openly proclaimed that they would win; and she added that, whether or not they asked for his help, the god would assist them in every way. This oracle was fulfilled in 404. But, even before this it had proved to be a trump card for the Spartan propagandists, particularly with neutral cities who had not yet thrown in their lot with either of the two great powers. On the other hand, of course, there was always the danger that an oracle of this sort would lower Apollo's prestige in Athens and amongst her allies.

When in accordance with the plan put forward by Pericles the peasants of Attica abandoned their farms to the Spartan invader and took refuge behind the Long Wall, they occupied the area below the Acropolis, sometimes called Pelasgicon in honour of the ancient Pelasgians, and sometimes Pelargicon, a favourite resort of seagulls. Now there was in existence a Pythian oracle which said: 'It is better not to live in Pelasgicon.' There was so little room in the city, however, that the peasants were obliged to settle there, and this undoubtedly aroused concern and protest amongst devout believers, for Thucydides notes: 'It seems to me that the oracle was fulfilled in a way quite contrary to what they expected, for one cannot

[1] Martin P. Nilsson, *La religion populaire dans la Grèce antique*, Paris, 1954, pp. 218–19.

suppose that the misfortunes of Athens arose from this spot having been profaned: it was occupied as a result of the necessity of war and this was not mentioned in the oracle, which only predicted that one day the spot would be occupied in connection with some untoward event.'

When they discovered that the enemy were laying waste the district of Acharnia, the great crowd of people confined within the walls of Athens demanded that the army should make a sortie and fight in open country—the very opposite of Pericles' plan. 'The people', says Thucydides, 'split up into hostile groups, some supporting the sortie, others, a minority, opposing it. Meanwhile the chresmologues were peddling all kinds of oracles and everyone was prepared to listen to those that supported his own opinion.'

When on top of all her other misfortunes Athens was struck by the terrible plague of 430–429, 'someone recalled, as happens in such circumstances, a prophecy that the old men declared they had heard in their youth: "When there shall be war against the Dorians, then too shall there be plague." Thereupon everybody began disputing whether the word in the oracle was really *loimos* (plague), or *limos* (famine), which differs by only one letter. However, since it was the plague they were suffering from, the majority were naturally convinced that the word in the oracle must have been *loimos*, for they adapted the meaning of the oracle to the misfortune they were experiencing.'

Finally, the most important part played by the oracle was in 415, the year that it was decided to undertake the Sicilian expedition, a supreme decision that was ultimately disastrous for Athens. The issue was bitterly disputed in the Assembly, Alcibiades and most of the younger men coming out in support of the enterprise, whereas Nicias (see above pp. 3–4) and those of equally ripe experience were extremely hesitant. Public opinion swayed this way and that, influenced by the various oracles that were given currency. Alcibiades' soothsayer prophesied that the Athenians would cover themselves with glory in Sicily. An ambassador who had been sent to consult the oracle of Ammon in Libya (see above p. 29) brought back the answer: 'The Athenians will take prisoner all the men of Syracuse.' Oracles to the opposite effect, one of which came from Dodona (see above p. 15), were hushed up. When the disastrous fate of the expedition ultimately became known in Athens, the politicians who had been in favour of it were attacked, but so too, according to Thucydides, were the 'chresmologues and soothsayers, who had roused the people by assuring them that they would be the masters of Sicily: they became objects of public scorn.'

In two of his comedies, *The Knights* (424 B.C.) and *The Birds* (414 B.C.) Aristophanes ridicules this use of oracles for political ends. In the earlier of the two plays the generals Nicias and Demosthenes, who are represented as slaves of Demos, a spoilt old man personifying the Athenian people, obtain oracles which confirm the authority of Cleon, the 'Paphlagonian' tanner; and later they discover another, which appears to imply that this leather-merchant will be succeeded as head of the Athenian government by a sausage-maker. A search is therefore instigated and they find a pork-butcher who turns out to be even more preposterous than Cleon, but as the oracles promise much more on his behalf it is he who emerges as the winner. Demos, having previously accepted Cleon's oracles, now puts his faith in those of the pork-butcher, who thus attains supreme authority.

In *The Birds*, when the city of Cloud-Cuckooland is founded, one of the first Athenians to offer his services is a chresmologue who propounds a number of meaningless oracles, whereupon the founder of the town quickly despatches him 'to the crows', or as we should say, to the devil.

In the fourth century the people of Athens as a whole continued to accept religion and therefore believed in the oracles, and even members of the ruling class like Xenophon still attached great importance to them. As we noted above (p. 59), before taking part in the expedition of the Ten Thousand, Xenophon, on the advice of his master Socrates, went to consult the Pythia, though the question he put to her was not the one suggested by the philosopher. In *Anabasis* he devotes considerable attention to oracular consultations, dreams and all kinds of presage. In any difficult situation he offers sacrifice and prays to the gods for guidance, as for example when he is offered the command of the expedition despite the fact that he had only joined it as a kind of war correspondent. It was from a dream that he found out the best way of crossing the Tigris; and on the way to Ephesus, when he heard the cry of an eagle, perched on a tree at the right-hand side of the road, his soothsayer assured him that this was a sign that all their difficulties would be crowned with success.

*   *   *

Nevertheless the fact that both before and after the Peloponnesian War the Delphic oracle had in the main supported Sparta was bound to create a lasting distrust of the Pythia among the Athenians. Despite this, in difficult questions affecting religion, tradition was so strong that the god of Delphi was still accepted as the court of final appeal. It is these two contradictory tendencies, I believe, that explain the unusual and quite surprising approach that Athens made to the Pythia in 352 B.C.

This arose from a discussion in the Assembly about the leasing of part of the plain that was dedicated to the goddesses of Eleusis, Demeter and Kore. As opinion was divided, it was decided that the matter should be referred to the highest religious authority in Greece, the Delphic oracle. The simplest thing would have been to send ambassadors to enquire of the god whether or not it was permissible to let these plots of land: instead of this, they set about it in the following complicated and scrupulously careful way.

A decree was passed, stipulating that the Secretary of the Council should procure two identical sheets of tin and have each of them engraved with a different question. The one would ask: 'Is it to the profit and advantage of the Athenian people that the archon-king should lease the plots within the bounds of the holy plain which are at present under cultivation, and use the income for building the entrance porch and for the upkeep of the temple of the two goddesses?' The other was to read: 'Is it to the profit and advantage of the Athenian people to leave uncultivated in honour of the two goddesses those plots of land within the bounds of the holy plain which are at present under cultivation?' Thus inscribed, the two sheets of tin were to be rolled up, wrapped in wool and, in full view of the people, be placed in a bronze vase by the Secretary. The Treasurers of Athens were then to bring into the Assembly two vases, one of gold and the other of silver; and the Secretary, having first shaken the bronze vase, was to take from it the two sheets of tin, putting the first into the golden vase and the second into the silver one. These were then to be carefully sealed and taken to the Acropolis by the Treasurers.

The decree continues: 'The people will then choose three citizens, one from the Council and the other two from the generality of the people, who shall proceed to Delphi and there ask the gods: "With regard to the sacred territory, should the Athenians act in accordance with the inscription in the golden vase or with that in the silver vase?" Then, when they have returned from waiting upon the god, the vases shall be brought to the Acropolis, where the oracle's reply shall be read to the people, as well as the inscriptions on both sheets of tin. And the procedure laid down in the inscription chosen by the god shall be accepted, as being to the greatest profit and advantage of the Athenian people.'[1]

Clearly, every possible precaution was to be taken. In the first place, when called upon to choose between the gold and silver vases lodged in the Acropolis, the Pythia would be completely ignorant of the issue at stake; and, in the second, neither the Athenians nor their ambassadors could know which of the two vases contained the inscription in favour of leasing the land. Thus it was impossible for the ambassadors to influence either the priests or the Pythia in either direction.

It is possible that in this case the consultation was by lot, in the manner described above (see pp. 17–18), and we cannot be sure that the Pythia would even have entered the *adyton*. Since the lot-oracle was assumed to reveal the will of the god, one

---

[1] This inscription was published by P. Foucart in the *Bull. Corr. hell.* 13 (1889), pp. 443–67. See also P. Amandry, *La mantique apollinienne à Delphes*, pp. 151–3.

would have thought it would have been simpler and less costly to have arranged to draw lots at Athens (as was done when electing most of the magistrates and judges), especially since it is clear that they distrusted the oracle at Delphi. But tradition was still too strong: questions relating to religious matters had in the last resort to be submitted to Pythian Apollo. Here, then, we have unmistakable evidence both of the growing suspicion of the Delphic priesthood felt in Athens and of the prestige which the Pythian oracle nevertheless still enjoyed. In order that the Athenian people might arrive at a decision about part of the sacred plain with a clear conscience, three ambassadors had to be sent all the way to Delphi, yet the question they put to the Pythia had to be in such an enigmatic form that she could not know what was involved. Thus although by consulting the oracle they seemed to be putting their trust in the irrational, at the same time the critical spirit of the Athenians was multiplying their doubts and reservations.

*   *   *

In 352 B.C., the year when this unusual consultation took place, Demosthenes was thirty-two years old and had already begun his political career. In the following year he was to deliver his first Philippic, the first blow in his policy of staunch opposition to the king of Macedonia. It was also the time of the third Holy War (356–346) which, like the Trojan War, was to last ten years. The Phocians, who lived in the country around Delphi, had occupied the sanctuary and forced the Pythia to declare herself in their favour, but the Amphictyons had replied by declaring war against them; and before long Philip, who regarded these sanguinary disputes as an excellent opportunity of establishing his influence in central Greece, intervened on the side of the Amphictyons, representing himself as Apollo's protector. By 346 the Phocians had been defeated, and Philip then joined the Council of the Amphictyons and presided at the Pythian Games.

In this same year Demosthenes concluded his speech *On the Peace* with these words: 'Would it not be folly and stupidity ... to go to war now for this shadow that is at Delphi?' He had in mind the proverb 'What's the good of fighting for the shadow of a donkey', and what he meant was 'What's the use of fighting for empty appearances, as though either the Amphictyony or the Delphic oracle were still of any importance?' Again, in about 340 B.C., when something happened that was considered to be a bad omen and an Athenian suggested in the Assembly that they should send an ambassador to consult the Pythia, Demosthenes replied, according to Aeschines: 'The Pythia is Philippizing.' By this he meant that she was taking Philip's side, as she had supported the Persians at the time of Xerxes' invasion and the Spartans during the Peloponnesian War.

In 339–338 B.C. Delphi was tragically involved in the political and military events which resulted in the defeat of the Athenians and Thebans, the last defenders of Greek liberty, at Chaeroneia, where they were overwhelmed by the Macedonian phalanx. This was, in fact, yet another Holy War, declared by the Amphictyons at the instigation of Aeschines against the Locrians of Amphissa who lived not far from the sanctuary; and once again it provided Philip with an excuse to enter central Greece with his army on the pretext of protecting Apollo.

There can be little doubt that political manipulation of the oracle, as well as the suspicion that certain predictions had been made in order to assist those states that were in a position to bring pressure to bear on the temple priesthood, were among the principal causes of the growing disillusionment of the Greeks with regard to divination, at least of the most enlightened of them. For a long time divination had been the most vital aspect of Greek religion: but if the spread of scepticism about the oracles helped to weaken belief in the gods, it is on the other hand equally true that the growth of religious belief dealt a severe blow at the faith in seers and oracles that the Greeks had once held.

5

DIVINATION AND PHILOSOPHY

To assume that Greek philosophers were as a whole opposed
to divination and, in a more general way, to the religion of
which divination was an integral part, would be short-sighted
and mistaken. On the contrary, many of the greatest of them—
Socrates, Plato, the Stoics, sought to provide rational justification for the phenomenon of prophecy. Thales of Miletus, a
physicist and astronomer who had scientifically predicted the
exact date of an eclipse of the sun, seems to have had a very
poor opinion of seers, to judge by the story Plutarch tells in
his *Symposium of the Seven Sages.* It is about a monster, which
a young shepherd insisted had been born of a mare: the upper
part of its body, as far as the neck and arms, was human, the
remainder was that of a horse, rather like the centaurs of
mythology. The seer Diocles looked upon it as a miracle
whereas Thales simply treated it with sceptical laughter. An
attitude of radical hostility to divination appears with Xenophanes of Colophon, for like Plato this philosopher not only
rejected anthropomorphism and all popular mythology, but
also the belief in divine providence which is the basis of belief
in oracles. As Cicero notes, Xenophanes was in fact the only
one of the ancients who completely denied divination.

On the other hand, Heracleitus of Ephesus and Empedocles
of Agrigentum attempted to provide a rational explanation of
prophetic ecstasy, which they accepted without reserve, though
at the same time expressing scant belief in inductive divination,
based upon material objects. Empedocles even claimed that he
himself was a kind of terrestrial divinity, with power to cure
disease as well as to utter prophecies.

But of all the pre-Socratic philosophers it was Democritus,
the founder of atomic theory, who gave the most detailed and

remarkable explanation of prophetic ecstasy; an explanation that was to be revived by Plato. According to him the human soul, a material entity, is composed of extremely subtle and mobile atoms. Thanks to an abnormal warmth and emotional susceptibility, the souls of madmen and of those with the gift of prophecy, are specially adapted to receive the material influences (*eidola*) emanating from other human beings and from the whole universe. When these emanations derive from those superior, though still material, beings, the gods, they imbue the soul either with poetic inspiration or with that revelation of hidden truth that constitutes the gift of prophecy.

With Anaxagoras of Clazomenae, the master and friend of Pericles, we have another case of a seer and a philosopher confronted by a prodigy, like Thales and Diocles. This time, the seer's name was Lampo, whom we have already met (p. 63). The incident occurred before Pericles had succeeded in defeating the aristocratic party, which was led by Thucydides, the son of Milesias, who was to be ostracized in 443. It is described by Plutarch in his *Life of Pericles*: 'One day, a ram's head with only one horn was brought to Pericles from his country estate. The soothsayer, Lampo, seeing that this horn grew strongly from the middle of the animal's forehead, declared that control of the two parties into which the country was split, that of Thucydides and that of Pericles, would ultimately fall to one man, he to whom this miracle had been vouchsafed. But Anaxagoras, having cut the skull in two, showed that the brain, instead of being in its normal place, was egg-shaped and had shifted to that part of the cranium beneath the root of the horn. At the time the opinion of those present supported Anaxagoras, but when shortly afterwards Thucydides was defeated and the entire management of affairs passed into the hands of Pericles, they believed Lampo!'

To which Plutarch, himself a philosopher, adds this curious commentary: 'For my part, I cannot see any reason why the philosopher and the seer could not have reached agreement, the one having correctly understood the cause, and the other the effect of the phenomenon. For the one professed to explain the causes and the modalities, and the other to prophesy in the light of what had occurred and what it signified. Those who maintain that to discover the cause of an omen is equivalent to destroying it do not realize that, in doing so, they reject not only the signs sent by the gods but also those produced by man-made instruments, such as the sound of cymbals, the light of torches or the shadow on a sun-dial, all of which are examples of things produced by virtue of a cause, but also in order to serve as signs.' This is typical of the mental subtlety with which the Greeks sometimes sought to reconcile the rational and the irrational.

*   *   *

We have already seen how greatly Socrates esteemed divination, particularly the oracle of Delphi. His disciple, Xenophon, says in his *Memorabilia*: 'This was the attitude that Socrates adopted towards his friends. He urged them to do those things where the result was certain to the best of their ability. But in those cases when the issue was in doubt he recommended divination, saying that if countries and families were to be well administered oracles were necessary. All knowledge is accessible to human intelligence except the most important part of it, and that the gods keep to themselves and men see only shadows.' For his own part Socrates always maintained that he had an inner voice, a kind of premonitory genius, which sometimes warned him seriously against undertaking some particular action. In his *Apologia*, Xenophon makes him say: 'How can it be said that, by insisting that a god's voice speaks in my ears and directs my behaviour, I am inventing new gods? For those who discover omens in human speech or in the song of a sparrow must base their conjectures on sound. And does anybody deny that the thunder speaks and is the most impressive of all auguries? Again, is it not by means of her voice that the Pythia, seated on her tripod, proclaims the god's will? In truth, everyone says and thinks as I do that the gods foresee the future and reveal it to whom they will. . . . That I do not lie about the gods is proved by the fact that I have already made known the divine purpose to several of my friends, and have never been found to be mistaken.'

Just as all Greek poets claimed to be descended from Homer, so from the fifth century onwards all philosophers admitted their debt to Socrates, even if some of them, the Cynics, for example, did not share the master's respect for divination. It was the Cynic Diogenes who said that, whenever he saw interpreters of dreams and soothsayers, and particularly the credulous people who believed in them, he was always tempted to think that man must be the stupidest creature in the world.

But for us the greatest of Socrates' disciples was undoubtedly Plato, whose reverence for Pythian Apollo was beyond question. He recognized only the official oracles that were published by the established sanctuaries; individual soothsayers and chresmologues he distrusted, looking upon many of them as charlatans. But for the oracles of Delphi, Dodona and Ammon he had nothing but praise, and he insisted that the whole religious life of his ideal city was to be based on the revelations stemming from these great mantic institutions, as may be clearly seen, for example, in Book v of *The Laws*. At the same time, Plato's philosophical system was firmly based on the primacy of reason and the method of the dialectic. How then, in his view, was it possible for seers and prophetesses, whose mode of comprehension is utterly different from that of philosophers, to apprehend the truth? His answer is to be found in the *Phaedrus*: he believed in a kind of intuitive knowledge quite distinct from the dialectic and indeed belonging to a lower order which was implanted in certain men and women by divine grace. This knowledge was so entirely different from the dialectic that it could only manifest itself when reason and commonsense were in eclipse: the state induced by the mystery cults, poetic inspiration, the exaltation of being in love and prophetic madness. This theory of 'possession', while it has the great advantage of associating divination with analogous phenomena instead of treating it in isolation, nevertheless remains extremely abstract and tells us little of the actual process of revelation.

For Plato the gods were always real, and it was not befitting their dignity to suppose that they themselves were directly responsible for the madness of poets and seers. It was easier to sustain the notion of divine transcendance if one assumed that the immediate agent of the state of inspiration was some kind of representative of the gods, half human and half divine; 'daimons' or 'genii'. This mantic demonology is clearly outlined in *The Symposium* by Diotima.

Was the ecstatic condition induced by the 'daimons' a purely spiritual state, or did it involve the entire human being, body and soul? Since it was related to Corybantic frenzy and manifested itself in violent physical symptoms, it must clearly have affected the whole organism. But in Plato's opinion, as may be seen from the *Timaeus*, there was one organ in particular that was affected by these phenomena, and that was the liver, doubtless because of the special significance of the liver in the form of divination based on the examination of the entrails of sacrificial animals (see above p. 12). By insisting upon the connection between the liver and prophetic ecstasy Plato was able to provide a physical explanation of possession different to that suggested by Democritus and the atomists. And it was this approach that Aristotle was to follow up.

Plato's devotion to the Delphic oracle was amply repaid. After his death, the Pythia—who, during his lifetime had proclaimed Socrates to be the wisest of men—was asked 'whether Plato's stele should be placed amongst the statues of the gods'; in other words, whether he was to be regarded as a semi-divine figure. She answered, thus proving that she was not incapable of gratitude, 'You are right to honour Plato, master of a divine doctrine.'

*   *   *

Aristotle's ideas about divination have given rise to contradictory interpretations. One thing at least is certain: in his opinion, the state of possession was connected with a definite physiological temperament, the melancholic temperament that is due to the influence of the black bile, which was supposed to have similar properties to the *pneuma*. 'Melancholics', people in whom the bile is too freely secreted, suffered from a condition comparable, in its effect on the blood, to fever or intoxication.

Does this mean that according to Aristotle prophetic madness was simply an illness to be explained by purely natural causes? That is not the opinion of P. Boyancé.[1] For one thing, it seems quite clear that Aristotle, like Plato, sharply distinguished between possession and mental illness; a passage in *Problems* states specifically: 'The Sibyls and the Bakis prophesy, not as a result of illness, but by virtue of their natural constitution.' Again, the black bile was thought to be a subtle kind of fluid belonging to a higher order than the four elements and analogous to the stars; its nature was comparable with that of the ether, the fifth element or 'quintessence', of celestial origin.

True, Aristotle appears to reject the notion of personal 'daimons' envisaged by Plato, but he attributes the powers of the 'daimons' and their intermediary role between man and god to nature. It is nature itself that is 'melancholic', that is to say 'daimonic'; and this is borne out by the fact that the bile, as a form of *pneuma*, is related to the noblest essence of the universe. Thus, despite appearances, Aristotle does not strip possession of its divine character, for his whole conception of the physical world retains a considerable religious, or as we should say metaphysical, element.

*   *   *

In the time of Alexander, though Plato's Academy and Aristotle's Lyceum still had disciples, two new schools were becoming known throughout the Greek world: the Stoa, from which the Stoics took their name, and the Garden founded by Epicurus. Their teachings were diametrically opposed, especially as regards belief in oracles. As Bouché-Leclercq has pointed out: 'No one wrote so much on this subject as the Stoics, and no other school of thought did more to strengthen belief in divination.' Previously many philosophers had accepted and even tried to explain intuitive divination, while rejecting divination by signs: the Stoics respected both methods. This is not surprising, since two doctrines basic to

[1] P. Boyancé, *Le culte des Muses chez les philosophes grecs*, Paris, 1937.

this teaching, their views on sympathy and on fatalism, were peculiarly favourable to a belief in divination.

For them, all creatures in the universe were united by 'universal, cosmic sympathy', so that there could be no fact that was not inevitably connected with the totality of facts, past, present and future. A man could not raise his finger, they used to say, without its effect being felt throughout the entire universe. Though these connections were hidden from the human mind, nevertheless they really existed. While it was not immediately obvious what connection there could be between the flight of a bird or the colour of an animal's liver and the winning of a battle, it was quite impossible that there should not be such a connection. The function of Providence, which the Stoics wholeheartedly believed in, was precisely to reveal to mankind these subsidiary relationships, these tenuous connecting threads that ordinary reason was powerless to grasp.

According to Cicero, the Stoics argued as follows: 'If the gods exist, and they do not reveal the future to mankind, it means either: (1) that they have no love for mankind; or (2) that they themselves are ignorant of what will happen in the future; or (3) that they do not consider it to be beneficial for men that they should foresee the future; or (4) that they believe it would detract from their own majesty if men were bound to have such knowledge; or (5) that men are incapable of such knowledge.' Having systematically refuted each of these five hypotheses, the Stoics concluded: 'If the gods do not reveal the future it is because there are no gods. But since the gods certainly do exist, therefore they reveal the future.' Thus, for them, belief in divination and belief in the gods were necessarily interdependent. In short, the Stoics claimed to have proved rationally what, during the centuries of faith, had been the universal belief of the peoples of antiquity.

Furthermore, their fatalism led the Stoics to think that the existing state of the world already contains, 'potentially', all its future states. One of them, Posidonios of Apamaeus, is reported by Cicero as saying: 'Reason compels us to believe that everything is governed by fate, that is to say by an order or sequence of interrelated causes and their necessary effects.

This is an everlasting truth, whose source is in eternity itself. . . . Thus fate is the eternal cause of all things, not simply according to the language of superstition, but according to the laws of nature; it is the cause that explains what has been done, what is being done, and what will be done in the future. Thus it is that, by observation, one can know what the consequences of each event will be. And it is this interlinking of cause and effect that is revealed through inspiration and dreams.'

To the objection that certain oracles had proved to be untrue, the Stoics' answer was that a seer could sometimes mistake a merely human idea for divine inspiration. 'Show us', they said, 'a single science where errors do not occur. Are we to refuse medicine the title of a science because sometimes it has been mistaken? Do pilots never get lost? Yet because many pilots have been shipwrecked it does not mean that the art of navigation is worthless. Are we to deny the value of strategy because generals have sometimes been defeated in battle?'

Compared with the dogmatic approach of the Stoics, the attitude of Epicurus and his disciples seems to have been one of radical scepticism. In their view of the world it was not fate that controlled the universe, but chance, *tyché*; nor did they believe in providence. Their gods (for the Epicureans were not atheists) held themselves remote from humanity and were but little concerned with the affairs of men. For the gods to have become involved would have destroyed their divine serenity.

In Plutarch's dialogue, *On the Pythian Oracles*, the Epicurean, Boethos, expresses himself as follows: 'With seers it is not so much a matter of predicting, as of simply speaking, or rather of throwing out and scattering heedless words into the infinity of possibilities. And since these words wander about haphazard, it happens that chance encounters them and coincides with them. For there is all the difference, I believe, between seeing something happen that has been spoken of and predicting what is going to happen. Prediction, which speaks with all the liability to error that is inherent in it of what has not yet come to pass, is not justified in expecting that it will be proved right by chance; nor can what happens later in any way demonstrate that the prediction was based on knowledge of what caused it to happen, for such is the infinity of possibilities that every kind of event may come about. In the course of time, which is as vast as the ocean, the Sibyls and Bakis have foretold every sort of event and misfortune: if it so happens that a number of them have come to pass, nonetheless at the time they were uttered their prophecies were lies, even if fortuitous circumstances should eventually appear to make them true.'

Thus, whereas for the Stoics the fact that a prediction was manifestly false did not logically destroy belief in oracles, equally logically, for the Epicureans, the fact that a prophecy proved to be correct did not substantiate the claims of divination.

* * *

Plutarch, to whose testimony we have so often appealed already, was both a philosopher and a priest of Pythian Apollo. As a philosopher, his ideas derived essentially from the system of the divine Plato, but he was also familiar with the teachings of the pre-Socratics, of Aristotle, the Stoics and the Epicureans. As priest of Apollo he was for many years the leading figure in the hierarchy surrounding the Pythia and, as such, had access to the *adyton*. He was thus doubly qualified, as no other ancient author was, to describe the oracle with full understanding.

In his time, it is true, under the Roman empire, the Greek oracles were no longer very flourishing or much frequented. In the first century B.C. even the oracle of Delphi suffered a temporary decline. Nevertheless during the time that Plutarch was the priest of Apollo (about A.D. 85–125) the Pythia was again receiving clients and the sanctuary was experiencing a kind of renaissance. Most of the other oracles in Greece, however, were silent, as may be gathered from the title of another dialogue that Plutarch devoted to divination, *On the Disappearance of Oracles*. Taking into account the conservative tendencies of religion, it seems likely that the rites as practised at Delphi had not substantially changed since the classical period.

The dialogue *On the Disappearance of Oracles* was written perhaps twenty or thirty years earlier than the dialogue *On the Pythian Oracles*, which definitely belongs to the very last years of Plutarch's life, and during this period his views about intuitive divination had changed considerably. The first is the work of a philosopher who is also a believer, in which he attempts to reconcile, not always successfully, his faith and his reason. In the second, he writes as a believer who regards philosophy as a means of exalting and publicizing his religious beliefs by refuting the objections of the sceptics. It would seem that, as he grew older, under the influence of the sacred city that had become his second home and in the sanctuary whose atmosphere must have increasingly appealed to anyone as naturally religious as himself, Plato had come to regard himself rather as a theologian than a philosopher; and, though he never rejected philosophy, more and more he came to see himself as the humble servant of theology, *ancilla theologiae*.[1] Essentially, both works were a defence of divination in general and of the Delphic oracle in particular, written as a reply to its critics and especially to the hostility of the Epicureans.

As its title suggests, *On the Disappearance of Oracles*, it first sets out to explain why so many mantic institutions had recently ceased to function. As the approach is primarily philosophical, it is the principle of intuitive divination that is discussed, since to understand why the oracles had collapsed one must first enquire how they originated: in short, what was the cause of prophetic inspiration. Two hypotheses are advanced in turn: one attributing the immediate cause of divination to 'daimons' or 'genii'; the other, to the fluid known as *pneuma*.

The germ of this mantic demonology is, as we have seen, already to be found in Plato's *Symposium*. But Plutarch insists on the fact that the 'daimons' responsible for divination, though they live much longer than men, are nevertheless mortal (for if they *were* immortal they would be gods); and, in a celebrated passage, he goes on to describe the death of the great god Pan, whom he considered to be one of these

[1] R. Flacelière, 'Plutarque et la Pythie' in the *Rev. Et. gr.* 56 (1943), pp. 37-9.

'daimons'. Some critics claim to see in this curious passage, as in the fourth Eclogue of Virgil, a presentiment of the end of paganism and the coming of Christianity, but so far no one has succeeded in providing a satisfactory, rational explanation of it. Plutarch goes on to say that when the presiding genius of a particular oracle happened to die the oracle's prophetic powers died with him, unless the gods chose to send another spirit to take his place.

Up to this point there is scarcely any reference to Delphi. On the other hand, as soon as Plutarch begins to expound his theory of a prophetic fluid he continually speaks of the Delphic oracle. It was, indeed, pretty generally accepted that the cause of the Pythia's ecstatic trance was some material exhalation, *pneuma*, that she breathed in as she sat upon her tripod above the chasm. This physical agent aroused some faculty of the soul, which 'thus warmed and burning discarded the reserve that normally inhibited ecstasy', that is to say, divine possession. What was involved here was not so much any positive action, as an inhibiting influence that swept away all obstacles and broke down the barriers between the god and his medium. The *pneuma* might have a violent and disturbing effect, even to the point of causing the Pythia's death (see p. 46). However, if the *pneuma* was the efficient secondary cause of divination, Pythian Apollo remained its primary cause, since it was from him that the *pneuma* was derived either directly or through the intermediary of the 'daimon' to whom he delegated his powers.

The whole tone of the second dialogue, *On the Pythian Oracles*, is entirely different. The speakers are on their way to visit the sanctuary of Apollo accompanied by guides who point out various statues and recite the oracles relating to them. The verse in which most of these oracles were written is so extremely mediocre that the question arises, how is it possible for Apollo Musagetes, the inspirer of the Pythia, to be so much less accomplished a poet than Homer or Hesiod? The Epicurean Boethos argues that this proves that Apollo refuses to believe in any kind of divination. But the Stoic Sarapion, one of Plutarch's friends, energetically defends Apollo, dismissing the literary taste of his contemporaries as perverted. Where-upon Theon, who may be regarded as Plutarch's spokesman, brings matters to a head by putting forward a theory of pro-phetic inspiration which has curious affinities with the ideas of certain Christian exegetists on the inspiration of the Bible and particularly of the prophetic books. According to Theon all the god does is to inspire the Pythia with a general vision of the truth and the future. The actual words in which she trans-mits this vision are ordinary human language chosen either by her or by the priests who attend her and subsequently edit the answers: 'For the god uses the Pythia to make known his thoughts in the same way that the sun [Apollo was also the sun god] uses the moon at night-time to reflect his rays. What he thus manifests to us are in truth his own thoughts, though by passing through a human soul and body they are adulter-ated.'

The form of the oracles was thus simply following the general law of evolution, from poetry to prose, in the same way as history and philosophy had done, but this was no reason for doubting the truthfulness of the god. In this dia-logue there is practically no reference to the theory of either 'daimons' or of '*pneuma*': it is Apollo himself who directly inspires his prophetess, without any intermediary or material agent. He does not dictate ready-made replies to her, but directly illuminates her mind through the phenomenon of possession.

The dialogue concludes with a glowing affirmation of the eternal fame of Delphi, despite so many signs of its decline. And Plutarch ends with a description of the renaissance of the Pythian sanctuary which was taking place in his own lifetime on the initiative of the emperor Hadrian, a renaissance in which he himself played a considerable part, both as the priest of Apollo and as the representative of the Amphictyon. No such revival would be possible, he declares, 'were it not for the presence of a god who confers his divine authority upon the oracle'; and he accuses the sceptics of being blind and childishly stupid. Thus the author of the *Parallel Lives* died in the firm conviction that the Delphic oracle would live for ever. He could not foresee that Apollo, whom he had served with such devotion, would, like his father Zeus and all the other Olympians, soon 'be wrapped in the purple shroud in which the dead gods sleep'.

CONCLUSION

We must now attempt to answer the question that we posed at the beginning of this booklet. There can be no doubt that the majority of the Greeks, like all the peoples of antiquity, continued to believe in oracles long after the classical century of Pericles, the period that saw the rise of the sophists and the awakening of rational criticism. Though Pericles himself, as well as Thucydides and later Demosthenes, seem to have been sceptical, most Athenians—and by no means the least of them, but men like Nicias and Xenophon—still put their faith in seers. In the fourth century, a philosopher of Plato's stature revered Pythian Apollo, the supreme god of prophecy. Even in the Hellenistic epoch and under the Roman empire, despite the negative attitude of the sceptics and the Epicureans, belief in oracles still found passionate defenders, particularly the Stoics and Plutarch. True, once a faith has to turn to apologists for its defence it is a sign that it has ceased to be either triumphant or incontestable. But for a long time to come astrology at least was still to be regarded as an infallible science.

My master Alain once said: 'Pythias, Sibyls, prophets are dreamers, who dream not for themselves but for us. They do not so much translate as directly express, by means of voice, gesture and attitude, the indivisible universe that reverberates within them. . . . And since the future depends upon the present, the fact that the Sibyl speaks and trembles involuntarily is enough to convince me that those things that concern me and of which I am ignorant are encompassed in her prophetic frenzy. But as to attempting to explain this, neither the Pythia nor Socrates nor anyone else has been able to do so; better to see in it what one pleases, and discover the prediction after the event. Hence these consultations with prophets and all these tricks with regard to the oracle, which in no way diminish man's respect. Consulting the oracle simply means looking for a reason for making a decision, when no reason is apparent. A man who makes up his mind by instinct is in a sense handing himself over to nature and trying to adapt himself to her; and in doing so he forgoes control of his own mind.

On the other hand, if he takes his problem to a seer, and listens to his advice, he can still choose. At least he will have a reason for his decision, which will serve as an excuse if later he finds he has made a mistake; and if he can put all the responsibility on a god, so much the better. These twists and turns, this subtle interplay of naivety and discretion, of reason and absurdity, are much closer to human reality than the prophecies we read about in books, clearly expressed, abstract, inflexible and humourless. There was very great maturity, genuine wisdom, in this Greek credulity, which, always and everywhere, was accompanied by its shadow, doubt.'[1]

Such, indeed, was the ambiguous position of the Greeks, torn between reason, the chosen guide that they knew to be inadequate, and their deep, instinctive belief in hidden powers. The very word 'mystery' is of Greek origin. The mysteries of Eleusis, like those of Dionysus and Orpheus, were man's answer to the terror of death and his ignorance of what lay beyond. Oracles helped mankind to find their way on this earth in the face of an unknown and threatening future. The fact that Socrates used to advise his disciples to consult the Pythia in no way detracts from his wisdom. After all, was it not she who proclaimed him to be the wisest of all men? In this at least she was not mistaken.

[1] Alain *Esquisses de l'homme*, Paris, 1938, pp. 66–7.

INDEX

89

Index

90

Index